TWAYNE'S WORLD AUTHORS SERIES
A Survey of the World's Literature

SPAIN

Janet W. Diaz, Texas Tech University

EDITOR

Rafael Dieste

TWAS 554

RAFAEL DIESTE

By ESTELLE IRIZARRY

Georgetown University

TWAYNE PUBLISHERS

A DIVISION OF G. K. HALL & CO., BOSTON

Printed on permanent/durable acid-free paper and bound
in the United States of America

First Printing

Frontspiece photograph of Rafael
Dieste by A. Buxán.

Library of Congress Cataloging in Publication Data

Irizarry, Estelle.
Rafael Dieste.

(Twayne's world authors series; TWAS 554: Spain)
Bibliography: p. 177–81
Includes index.
1. Dieste, Rafael—Criticism and interpretation.
PQ6607.I36Z72   868'.6'209   79–9809
ISBN 0–8057–6396–1

To Professor Rafael Supervía,
noble Spaniard in America

Contents

About the Author

Estelle Irizarry, Professor of Spanish and Spanish-American litera-
ture at Georgetown University, holds a B.A. degree from Montclair
State College, an M.A. from Rutgers University and a Ph.D. from
The George Washington University.

Professor Irizarry is the author of *Teoría y creación literaria en
Francisco Ayala* (Madrid: Editorial Gredos, 1971), an annotated
critical edition of Ayala's *El rapto, Fragancia de jazmines y Diálogo
entre el amor y un viejo* (Barcelona: Editorial Labor, 1974), a
scholarly edition of *Martín Fierro* (Zaragoza: Clásicos Ebro, 1975),
La inventiva surrealista de E. F. Granell (Madrid: Insula, 1976), a
critical edition of César Tiempo's *Clara Beter: Versos de
una . . .* (Buenos Aires: Editorial Rescate, 1977), *Francisco Ayala*
(Boston: Twayne Publishers, 1977), and *La broma literaria en
nuestros días* (New York: Eliseo Torres, 1979).

Professor Irizarry has written a monthly section on Hispanic
culture in the United States for the Mexican magazine *Nivel* since
1970 and has contributed many studies of Spanish and Spanish-
American literature to scholarly journals such as *Insula, Cuadernos
Hispanoamericanos, Cuadernos Americanos, Papeles de Son Arma-
dans, La Torre, Espiral,* and *Inti.* She has also written chapters in
several volumes of collective criticism published in Spain, Mexico,
and the United States.

Preface

The purpose of this book is to provide readers of English with a critical analysis of the complete works to date of Rafael Dieste, an extraordinary, versatile writer who after two decades of exile returned to Spain in 1961 and since that time has been increasingly recognized as one of the country's finest writers. Not since Unamuno and Machado has Spanish literature been accompanied by such profound philosophical motivation.

It may seem ironic that this, the first monograph on Rafael Dieste, should appear in English, but then the history of Spain in this century is filled with similar surprises, the most tragic being the Civil War of 1936 which sent a whole generation of emerging writers into exile in Latin America, England, and the United States, making them ipso facto "world authors," far from their somewhat isolated peninsular environment. Because many emigrants found themselves among fellow countrymen in Argentina, Mexico, Puerto Rico and other centers, they did not suffer the anguish of what Juan Marichal called the "second exile," that of alienation from their Spanish language. Like Dieste in Buenos Aires, they continued to write in their native tongue finding readers and critics, although not in the same measure as under more normal circumstances.

In the early 1960's, with some relaxation of hostility toward those who had left Spain, some of the lost generation began to visit their homeland, even establishing their homes there. Rafael Dieste made the difficult decision to leave Argentina in 1961 and quietly returned to his family's residence on the western coast of Galicia, in his native Rianxo. His reincorporation into the intellectual life of Galicia was swift and enthusiastic, but then he had been one of the greatest writers in the vernacular in prewar days. His reemergence as an author of national stature, however, was slower, perhaps because he resided and continues to reside in Rianxo and La Coruña, far from the publishing centers of Spain, Madrid and Barcelona.

Although Eugenio G. de Nora and José Marra-López discovered Dieste for the Spanish public in important books published respectively in 1962 and 1963, his works were virtually unknown and unavailable to Spanish readers at that time. His 1974 reedition of *Stories and Inventions of Félix Muriel*, received with superlatives when first published in Buenos Aires in 1943, was heralded in Spain as one of the most extraordinary and unique literary creations of our times. It was recognized that the book defied traditional concepts of genre, and it would seem from many of the reviews that it defied analysis, too. This study considers *Félix Muriel* at great length because of its importance not only in Dieste's total creation but in Spanish letters in general. But Dieste is not the author of only one book, however outstanding. He has excelled in several genres: narrative, theater, poetry, and essays, and his interests span literature, language, painting, philosophy, and mathematics—all articulated in his inventions and unified by his particular vision of life.

While many articles have appeared in the Spanish press, they have been chiefly in the form of laudatory reviews of specific works with few attempts at exegesis. The majority of these reviews have been written by fellow Galicians, but in recent years, some of Dieste's works have been studied in greater depth outside Galician circles in prestigious periodicals and journals, such as *Insula, Cuadernos Hispanoamericanos, Destino, Triunfo,* and *Cuadernos para el Diálogo*. His theater and poetry, however, have been generally unapproached by critics beyond the initial commentaries appearing at the time of publication. As for his writings in the vernacular, they have not been translated into Spanish and have received limited attention, almost exclusively by Galician critics. A chapter on Dieste's essays on various themes is included as a vital adjunct to a fuller appreciation of his primarily literary works.

I am indebted to Rafael Dieste for making available to me his private files of articles, reviews, and correspondence. Many of these secondary sources are not easily found in this country or even in Spain due to the limited circulation of some newspapers and journals. He also was kind enough to provide copies of publications which have been out of print for years. Special recognition should be accorded to the writer's wife Carmen Muñoz de Dieste for her prodigious organization of innumerable secondary materials, her efficient handling of correspondence, and warm words of encouragement—all of which facilitated my work and made it a pleasant task.

Translations of texts from Galician and Spanish into English are mine, but given Dieste's knowledge of English, he was able to offer valuable suggestions and indications regarding precision of translation, for which I am grateful.

In the preparation of this volume which involves a great variety of genres and themes, attention has been given to reiterated motifs and concerns to point out the underlying organic unity of the works studied. It is hoped that this book will contribute to a rediscovery of Dieste's lesser-known works as well as a deeper understanding of his most famous ones, will lead to an appreciation of the Galician spirit and consciousness in his personality and works and, above all, will stimulate further studies by scholars. Although this is the first at-length analysis of Rafael Dieste's writings, it does not purport to be exhaustive. And finally, it is my sincere hope that this book will hasten the process, already initiated, of according Rafael Dieste the prominent place he deserves in the Spanish intellectual history of ideas, literature, and culture in the twentieth century.

ESTELLE IRIZARRY

Georgetown University

Chronology

1899   January 29: Rafael Dieste born in Rianxo, La Coruña Province (Spain). Primary schooling in Rianxo.

1914   Begins Santiago Normal School.

1917   Trip to Tampico (Mexico). Purchases return trip with proceeds of a literary prize.

1918   Return to Galicia, with a long stopover at Havana when the ship is quarantined.

1919   Completes Santiago Normal School. September 26: father's death.

1921   Begins military service in Santiago. Sent to Morocco for two years following the disaster at Annual.

1925   Journalist in Vigo, first with *Galicia* and later as editorial secretary of *El Pueblo Gallego*.

1926   Publishes *Dos arquivos do trasno*.

1927   Play *A fiestra valdeira* published.

1928   Several months' stay in London, then Paris.

1930   First edition of *Viaje y fin de don Frontán*.

1932   Creation of the Guignol Theater of the Republican Misiones Pedagógicas.

1933   Publication of the first edition of *Rojo farol amante*.

1934   *Quebranto de doña Luparia y otras farsas* published. September 3: marries Carmen Muñoz Manzano.

1935   Studies theater and staging in France and Belgium on a grant from the Junta de Ampliación de Estudios en el Extranjero. Travels with Carmen to Holland, Italy, and France, where he writes *La vieja piel del mundo*. September: returns to Rianxo; December: travels to Madrid.

1936   Reincorporation into the Republican government's Pedagogical Missions. *La vieja piel del mundo* published just before the outbreak of the Spanish Civil War on July 18. Participation in the organization and activities of the Alliance of Anti-Fascist Writers. Directs the Teatro Español, Madrid. *Al amanecer* performed.

1937 Founding of *Hora de España* with Antonio Sánchez Barbudo and Juan Gil-Albert. *Nuevo retablo de las maravillas* published. October: takes charge of the magazine *Nova Galiza* in Barcelona.

1938 March: *Al amanecer* published in *Hora de España*. November: volunteers for the Eastern Front. Shares with Sánchez Barbudo the editorship of *El Combatiente del Este*.

1939 February: Leaves Spain after the fall of Barcelona. In France confined in Saint-Cyprien Concentration Camp for twenty days, and released owing to the influence of French authors; goes to Poitiers, then The Hague and Rotterdam. Sets out for Montevideo, Uruguay, arriving in June. July 12: Buenos Aires.

1940 Literary director of the publishing department of Atlántida in Buenos Aires until 1948. Second edition of *Rojo farol amante*.

1941 Publishes *Colmeiro. Breve discurso acera de pintura con el ejemplo de un pintor*.

1943 Publication of *Historias e invenciones de Félix Muriel*.

1944 Dieste's mother dies at an advanced age in Rianxo.

1945 *Viaje, duelo y perdición* published.

1948 Publishes *Luchas con el desconfiado*.

1949 Travels to Belgium, Holland, Italy, France, and England.

1950 October: lecturer in Spanish Language and Literature at Cambridge University for two years.

1952 May: goes to Paris, then to Monterrey, Mexico. Professor of Spanish Language and Literature at the Instituto Tecnológico y de Estudios Superiores, Humanities Section, in Monterrey for two years.

1954 Returns to Buenos Aires; resumes work with Atlántida.

1955 Publishes *Nuevo tratado del paralelismo*.

1956 *Pequeña clave ortográfica*.

1961 Returns to Spain, residing in Rianxo.

1965 Dual residency in La Coruña and Rianxo. Publishes *Diálogo de Manuel y David*.

1966 Begins lecturing tour in various cities with travelling exhibit of Carlos Maside's paintings and different cultural activities with the Laboratorio de Formas of Galicia.

1967 Publication of *¿Qué es un axioma?*.

1970 Received into the Royal Galician Academy as a regular member.

Chronology

1971 Publication of *A vontade de estilo na fala popular*.
1973 Publishes definitive edition of *Dos arquivos do trasno*.
1974 New edition of *Historias e invenciones de Félix Muriel*.
1975 *Testamento geométrico* published.

CHAPTER 1

A Voyage Begins . . .

R AFAEL Dieste frequently refers to his writings in terms of sea
voyages undertaken with a sense of adventure and mystery
toward uncertain destinations, and invites his readers to share the
experience. Marine metaphors abound in his narrative, poetry,
theater, and essays, not as mere adornment but rather as an integral
part of his view of life, influenced without doubt by his having lived
in his youth and later years overlooking the sea in his native Galician
town of Rianxo.[1] Dieste himself provides the suggestion, describing
his life and times in terms of a free-sailing voyage in a poem from
Rojo farol amante (Loving Red Lantern):

No me verás triste	You will not see me sad
sino maravillado.	but rather in wonder.
En barco de nacer	On the ship of birth
y morir, embarcado.	and death embarked.[2]

This ship has much of the mysterious attraction of another which,
captained by a strange sailor and graced by a fascinating song,
captivated the legendary Count Arnaldos in a famous old Spanish
ballad. Dieste's voyage has taken him across oceans, and while he
has always tried to inquire into the nature of the journey, it seems
that he would not want to take away any of its essential mystery.

I *Childhood*

The point of departure is Rianxo, a small coastal town on the Ría
de Arosa (Inlet of Arosa) on the western coast of Galicia, in the
province of La Coruña. Rafael Dieste was born January 29, 1899, a
year after the disastrous defeat of Spain and the loss of her last
colonies in America in the Spanish-American War. It was a trauma
which launched a magnificent generation of writers of the caliber of
Unamuno, Machado, Azorín, Baroja, and Valle-Inclán, known as

17

the Generation of 98 and which touched off a conscientious and sometimes auguished examination of the "problem of Spain."

Dieste's father, Eladio Dieste Muriel (1845–1919) had hoped to be a military staff officer, but finding himself past the prescribed age and attracted by adventure, he went to America to join his brother Eduardo, a ranch owner in Uruguay whose motives for emigrating there are not known. Eladio Dieste Muriel married Olegaria Gonçalvez Silveira, the daughter of Uruguyan ranch owners, there fathering four children; Enrique, Eladio, Eduardo, and Antonio, all taken to Spain when very young. After the return of Eladio Dieste Muriel to his native Galicia, three more children were born, Olegaria and Manuel in Pontevedra, and Rafael, the youngest, in Rianxo. In later years the family would again be spread out geographically, with Antonio and Manuel residing in Mexico, the others (except Rafael) in Uruguay. Rafael, exiled in Argentina, later returned to Spain.

Young Rafael Dieste attended primary school in Rianxo and in 1914 entered Santiago Normal School to study to be a teacher.

II   Emergence of a Young Writer

Philosophy, art, and literature were from adolescence among Rafael Dieste's major interests. In 1917 he travelled from his native Rianxo to Mexico but, moved by nostalgia, returned home the following year with the proceeds of a literary prize. Back in Galicia he completed his studies for a teaching degree from Santiago Normal School in 1919. In September of that year his father died. Dieste took an active part in the efforts of the young generation to foment Galicia's artistic expression in the vernacular, writing stories which would be published in *Dos arquivos do trasno* (From the Goblin's Archives). In 1921, he began military service, which was extended because of the military campaign against the Rifs in Morocco, following the disastrous retreat of Spanish forces defeated in Annual. After two years there, Dieste returned to Galicia and engaged in a career in journalism with *Galicia* and then *El Pueblo Gallego* as Editorial Secretary, writing over 250 articles both in Galician and Spanish which he hopes to publish some day in an anthology. He also published stories, which appeared as a collection, *From the Goblin's Archives*, in 1926. The book was enthusiastically received by readers and critics, as was his play in Galician, *A fiestra valdeira* (The Empty Window), the following year.

In 1928 Dieste spent a few months in London at the home of his brother Eduardo, who was Consul General there, and later that year travelled to Paris where as a "studious Bohemian" he enjoyed reading, taking long walks, and visiting museums. Two years later the first edition of *Viaje y fin de don Frontán* (Journey and End of Don Frontán) was published.

III   Contributions to the Spanish Republic

With the advent of the Spanish Republic in 1931, as the result of peaceful elections following the seven-year military dictatorship of Primo de Rivera, sanctioned by Alfonso XIII who accepted exile soon after the elections, an intense campaign was launched to raise the cultural level of the common people. Dieste was invited by Pedro Salinas to join the Misiones Pedagógicas (Pedagogical Missions) founded by the liberal educator Manuel Bartolomé Cossío. Although the purpose was to bring the best of the city to the country, long ignored by the Spanish governments, the "missionaries" themselves were enriched by the best of the country as they became better acquainted with remote parts of their land:

Lectures, movies, theater, travelling museums, dialogues, constituted the principal instruments and means of expression of the Missions, always received with delight in the villages and towns, and which left behind fertile nostalgia, new orientation, and strong desires to join in the great renovation of Spain.[3]

Dieste was assigned the task of organizing the Guignol (Puppet) Theater of the Missions, which began its activities in 1932. The author wrote and improvised numerous farces of his own creation or related to popular traditions. He also participated actively in all aspects of the craft, including stage and puppet design. His volume *Quebranto de doña Luparia y otras farsas* (The Breaking of Doña Luparia and Other Farces), published in 1934, reflects his intense creative energy during this period. In the Guignol Theater Dieste received the collaboration of Fernández Mazas, Ramón Gaya, Urbano Lugrís, Miguel Prieto, and later, Luis Cernuda. He also worked with María Zambrano, Antonio Sánchez Barbudo, Lorenzo Varela, Arturo Serrano Plaja, Eduardo Vicente, and Antonio Ramos. The experience of visiting towns, villages, and cities together provided for a constant exchange of views on matters personal, civic, and literary, which gave a special character to the group.

Dieste met Carmen Muñoz Manzano, an Inspector of Primary Education in Cáceres, while the Missions group he directed was on tour in Valencia de Alcántara (a town near the Portuguese border), where she had gone with the Chief Inspector, Juvenal de Vega, to offer their services. Carmen joined the group while the Missions stayed in that area. Six months later they were married, on September 3, 1934. Dieste's book of plays *Viaje, duelo y perdición* (Journey, Duel, and Perdition) is dedicated "to Carmen, friend of wild flowers."

In 1935, sponsored by the Junta de Ampliación de Estudios en el Extranjero (Board for Extension Studies Abroad), Dieste travelled to Belgium and France to study literary and technical aspects of theater. He extended his travels and with Carmen visited Holland and Italy. While abroad he contributed to the magazine *P. A. N.*, supported by his brother Eduardo and directed by José Otero Espasandín. His essays "Revelación y rebelíon del teatro" (Revelation and Rebellion of the Theater), "Una semblanza de Buscón poet" (A Portrait of the Poet Buscón), and the movie script for "Promesa del viejo y de la doncella" (The Promise of the Old Man and the Maiden) were written during this period.

Dieste wrote *La vieja piel del mundo: Sobre el origen de la tragedia y la figura de la historia* (The Old Skin of the World: On the Origin of Tragedy and the Figure of History) in August of the same year, 1935, while in Paris. As Carmen informs us, he read avidly and took notes for the report he was to present to the Board on his trip in a small study in the Place Jussieu near the Botanical Gardens. His notes began to take an unexpected turn in depth and style asserting their complete autonomy as an expression of something latent in his spirit, and so the book came to be written in fifteen days without rest. The title sprang from a dream of Carmen's in which she was seated before an enormous book of blank pages with a quill pen, and when asked by her husband what she was writing, she answered, "The Old Skin of the World." Dieste was delighted with this title and kept as a subtitle one of the earlier provisional titles he had discarded. He finished the book in twenty-three hours straight, scarcely aware that the time had elapsed. According to Carmen, in this book as well as in others, the author followed his customary manner of writing without consulting reference books; strangely enough, subsequent reference verifies the accuracy of his intuition and memory.

Dieste could have requested a renewal of his scholarship but, moved by vague premonition of trouble in Spain, he returned to Rianxo in September and in December travelled to Madrid. He was about to promote a transformation of the Pedagogical Missions that would change the scholarship foundation without altering its spirit into a Board for Extension Studies in the Interior when war broke out on July 18, 1936. Pedro Salinas's company Signo had just published *The Old Skin of the World*. Most of the edition was destroyed in a bombing attack on the capital. In September Dieste became director of the Teatro Español of Madrid where *Al amanecer* was performed.

The following year in Valencia, with Antonio Sánchez Barbudo and Juan Gil-Albert, Dieste founded the journal *Hora de España* (Spanish Hour), an attempt to stimulate and preserve culture in this dark hour. With the adherence from the start of the great poet-philosopher of the Generation of 98, Antonio Machado, the *Hora de España* Group or "Missionaries" included not only the founders, Manuel Altolaguirre and Ramón Gaya, but later Arturo Serrano Plaja, Angel Gaos, María Zambrano, and E. Casal Chapí. They worked hard so that the Republic was able to sustain a broad and free cultural expression relevant to that time along with its civic and heroic efforts. It became urgent to support actively the cause of the Republicans or Loyalists beseiged by Franco's Nationalists supported by Italian and German troops. Dieste's *Nuevo retablo de las maravillas* (New Spectacle of Wonders), an anti-Nationalist take-off on a Cervantes farce, appeared in the January 1937 issue of *Hora de Espana*. In October, Dieste assumed directorship of the magazine *Nova Galiza* (New Galicia) from Castelao. His contributions to this bilingual publication (Galician and Castilian) appeared signed, anonymously, or with the pseudonym Félix Muriel. Later Dieste volunteered for the Eastern Front where he shared with Sánchez Barbudo the editorship of *El Combatiente del Este* (The Eastern Combatant).

IV   *The Voyage to America*

The rest is history, the fall of Spain to the Nationalists and the emigration and dispersion of a whole generation of Spanish intellectuals. In February 1939, after the fall of Barcelona and the defeat of the Eastern Army, Dieste left Spain and was confined on arrival in France to the Saint-Cyprien Concentration Camp in the eastern Pyrenees. As an immediate epilogue, almost the entire *Hora de España* Group was detained there, an experience which Juan Gil-Albert recounts in *Memorabilia* (Barcelona: Tusquets Editor, 1975).

While Dieste was leaving Spain with the Eastern Army, Carmen abandoned Barcelona only a few hours before the arrival of the Nationalist troops. In a terrible bombardment of Figueras she was wounded in the arm and her friend, the wife of Ramón Gaya, was killed. Carmen managed to escape to France carrying the infant daughter of her friend and, leaving the child in the care of Corpus Barga's family, she entered La Pitié Hospital in Paris for two months for treatment of the infected arm. It was there that she learned that her husband was in the Saint-Cyprien Concentration Camp.

Dieste, freed owing to the influence of French writers (with the diligent cooperation of the English Quakers), was permitted to go to Poitiers where together with Sánchez Barbudo, Serrano Plaja, Gaya, and Gil-Albert, he was the guest of the French author Jean Richard Bloch in his country villa La Mérigotte. The odyssey took him from France to The Hague and then Rotterdam, leaving for Montevideo on the cargo ship *Alwaki*, which carried twenty passengers, and going on to Buenos Aires where he arrived July 12, 1939.

Our author established himself in Buenos Aires where he lost no time in undertaking new intellectual and cultural pursuits. From early 1940 to mid 1948 he was literary director of the editorial department of Atlántida. He found that the Galician emigrants in Buenos Aires (among them Lorenzo Varela, Arturo Cuadrado, Otero Espasandín, Eduardo Blanco Amor, Emilio Pita, Colmeiro, Seoane, and occasionally Castelao) formed an active and cohesive group. There were *tertulias* (gatherings) in the Café Tortoni and other events which brought them together with Argentine and Spanish intellectuals but probably also stimulated memories of their common native land. Dieste published several books in the Argentine capital: *Rojo farol amante* (Loving Red Lantern) in a second enlarged edition (1940), *Colmeiro* (1941), *Historias e invenciones de Félix Muriel* (Stories and Inventions of Félix Muriel, 1943), *Viaje, duelo y perdición* (Journey, Duel, and Perdition, 1945), *Luchas con el desconfiado* (Struggles with the Distrustful.

1948), and translations, adaptations, and various other works. He also lectured and taught in various academic and cultural centers in Buenos Aires, La Plata, and Montevideo.

Dieste crossed the Atlantic once more, in 1949, to visit several European countries with his wife (Belgium, Holland, Italy, and France) in an official Commission of Studies to inform the Museum of Modern Art of Montevideo about contemporary European painting. They visited galleries and museums in the company of their friends, the writer Esther de Cáceres and her husband the distinguished psychiatrist Alfredo Cáceres. In September, Carmen went to Spain for a three-week trip to visit family while Rafael, unwilling to break his exile, stayed in London; there he met J. B. Trend, Head of the Spanish Department of Cambridge University, who invited him to serve as Lecturer in Spanish Language and Literature at that university for a two-year period.

Following these years at Cambridge, Dieste and his wife went to Paris in May 1952, where they met with friends, Colmeiro, Scoane, María Zambrano, Serrano Plaja, Ferrater Mora, Octavio Paz, and the Hispanists Jean Cassou, Jean Camp, Marcel Bataillon, Sarrail, Matilde Pomés, and Verdevoye. He then went to Monterrey, Mexico, as professor of Spanish language and literature at the Institute of Technological and Higher Studies (Humanities Division) for two years and lectured on aesthetics and art theory at the University of Nuevo León.

In 1954 Dieste returned again to Buenos Aires to resume his editorial work with Atlántida, publishing in 1955 *Nuevo tratado de paralelismo* (New Treatise on Parallelism) and the following year *Pequeña clave ortográfica* (Small Orthographic Key). In 1959 Citania published Dieste's new version of *The Empty Window*. Perhaps upon returning to this early work (originally published in 1927), he realized how ironically prophetic it was and how the Galician seascape cut out of the protagonist's portrait (the empty window of the title) was now that of the author himself. In any case, he decided to take leave of his many friends and admirers in the Argentine capital and to return, after an absence of over twenty years, to Rianxo.

V *The Return*

The decision to return to Spain was not an easy one and was reached, according to Carmen, when it became evident to Dieste that continuing his exile served no useful political purpose. The artist Luis Seoane's farewell to Dieste was broadcast on the program "Galicia Emigrante" (Galicia Abroad) on July 30, 1961, in which he observed, "nostalgia for Galicia is in large measure responsible for the coming and going through the world of her children, who do not find a propitious atmosphere in any land that is not their own." He spoke of the pain of wanting to give life to that faraway world "in narrative, in poem or in picture, and to extract from memory the characters, the colors, and the life belonging to bygone times."

After well over two decades of absence the sailor returned to his place of origin and established himself once more in his ancestral home, an old stone house whose façade displays a heraldic family crest and whose glass-enclosed balconies overlook the Bay of Rianxo. For the traveller the seascape of his "empty window" was restored. Even after the return, Dieste and his wife were not sure about staying there, although greeted with cordiality. There was a period of strangeness and difficult adjustment and they refused to take part in any activity which could be construed as conformity or collaboration with the Franco regime. Carmen even waited three years before requesting reincorporation into the Inspection of Primary Education for fear of meeting with an atmosphere of rigidity, which fortunately did not occur. In those early days of their return the cultural reopening of Spain was still far off.

Evidently stimulated by the renewed contact with a familiar and yet changed environment and also in response to the requests of old literary friends, Dieste undertook a new edition of his very first book of Galician stories and published in 1962 *From the Goblin's Archives*, whose original edition dated from 1926. A final revision would be made in 1973. Dieste was received as a regular member of the Royal Galician Academy on April 18, 1967. His address *A vontade de estilo na fala popular* (Stylistic Motivation in Popular Speech) was published in book form in 1971 with an accompanying study by Domingo García-Sabell.

Since his return to Spain, Dieste has mainly dedicated himself to philosophical and mathematical reflections: *Diálogo de Manuel y David* (Dialogue of Manuel and David, 1965), *¿Qué es un axioma?* (What Is an Axiom?, 1967), and *Testamento geométrico* (Geometric Testament, 1975), as well as to lecturing and writing about Galician artists. He also participates actively in the Laboratorio de Formas de Galicia (Laboratory of Forms of Galicia). His prestige in his *"patria chica"* (little homeland or region) was not long in coming, but there was still the process of rediscovery by the general Spanish-reading public outside of Galicia. His works had been inaccessible to the latter for years. The rediscovery was facilitated by Eugenio G. de Nora's *La novela española contemporánea* (The Contemporary Spanish Novel, 1962) and by José Marra-López's *Narrativa española fuera de España* (Spanish Narrative Outside of Spain, 1963), with their enthusiastic appraisal of Dieste's works. Above all, a new edition of *Stories and Inventions of Félix Muriel* in 1974 elicited spectacular critical response. Interviews and articles about Dieste now appear regularly in major Spanish journals as well as in periodicals published in Galicia.

The personal qualities of Dieste most often mentioned by friends and critics are dignity, *hidalguía* (somewhat akin to nobility of spirit), courtesy, modesty, and wisdom. He has always been reserved in public, avoiding the limelight but generous in giving of himself in promoting cultural activities. His friends speak of his integrity and rectitude. His writings reveal the importance of friendship, sincerity, and communication, and this is evident even in the long-distance correspondence which constituted the basis of this critic's acquaintance with Dieste. And now, even in port, the indefatigable Galician sailor actively continues his intellectual and cultural voyages, still seeing "the old skin of the world" with the fresh and childlike wonder of his extraordinary Félix Muriel.

CHAPTER 2

Stories From the Goblin's Archives

R AFAEL Dieste's first published book, *Dos arquivos do trasno* (From the Goblin's Archives), a collection of short stories written in Galician which appeared in 1926, strangely became the first work published after his return to Spanish soil as a second edition (1963) containing some revisions and additions. Finally, attesting to the essential unity which with this author transcends circumstance and time, a third and definitive edition was published in Vigo in 1973. The second edition included "O neno suicida" (The Child Who Committed Suicide), "Na morte de Estreliña" (On the Death of Estreliña), "O grandor do mundo" (How Great the World Is), and "Espanto de nenos" (Children's Fright) which originally accompanied his play *A fiestra valdeira* (The Empty Window) in 1927 as a sort of epilogue providing local color. Also included were six stories of the same period which had appeared in *El Pueblo Gallego* and two stories written outside of Galicia in the 1950's, "Un conto de Reis" (A Story About Kings), commissioned by the British Broadcasting Company in London, and "De cómo veu a Rianxo unha balea" (How a Whale Came to Rianxo), written for a magazine of the Rianxo Society in Buenos Aires.

There are not many authors who can take up the pen at age sixty-four to contribute to the development of a book published at age twenty-seven. The fact that it is virtually impossible to distinguish the stories of more recent vintage from the original components of the volume is convincing proof of this author's ability to integrate diverse manifestations of his thought and creativity in a vital and organic whole. In the same way that he returned to his native Rianxo after war and exile, he returned to his first literary creations, finding in them "a unity that deserved to be exposed or configurated as such" and introducing changes "suggested directly by the new contact with the people and the new immersion in the linguistic climate of the Galician people." [1] The final version of *Dos arquivos do trasno* (From the Goblin's Archives), then, is a combination of early insight and later intuition, of foresight and hindsight interwoven so effectively that it reflects the basic unity of its author's individuality and identity.

The literary atmosphere of the late 1920's when these stories were first published was described by Roberto Blanco Torres in a 1930 article entitled "The New Galician Generation." This generation of young writers was, according to the author, not particularly dissident but neither did it accept the vanguard modes, the rhetorical acrobatics, of those who were writing in Spanish, preferring to foment a spirit of consciousness with regard to Galicia. Blanco Torres cites Dieste's books in Galician as "the culminating moment of the vernacular literary flowering of these last years" and calls the author "the most outstanding figure of the present generation." [2] He particularly admires Dieste's philosophical bent, psychological vigor, intensity, human emotion, aesthetic excellence, and sense of setting.

While Dieste's work does not fall easily into arbitrary categories, there are some broad orientations in the stories in *From the Goblin's Archives* which reveal similar aesthetic, atmospheric, or thematic concerns.

I *Stories of Mystery*

Galician literature has traditionally dealt with the strange, mysterious, and even supernatural, as may be seen in the works of Rosalía de Castro, Ramón del Valle-Inclán, the contemporary poet Alvaro Cunqueiro, and the Surrealist writer E. F. Granell. This vein is amply represented in *From the Goblin's Archives,* as the title itself suggests. Dieste integrates everyday reality and the unusual in one single reality not dependent upon the miraculous or supernatural but rather upon the ability to perceive the marvellous. Domingo García-Sabell seems to appreciate this aspect of the author's creativity when he refers to "the total communication of total reality" in which logical and "translogical" reality are blended into a unified structure.[3]

In the story "En col da morte de Bieito" (On the Death of Bieito), the narrator tells of hearing the dead Bieito stir within the coffin he and others are carrying to the cemetery. He speculates about how celebrated he would be if in fact Bieito were found to be alive but also how he would be ridiculed if the opposite were true, so he says nothing. After a day of doubt and remorse he sneaks into the cemetery at night and, with his ear trained to the ground, hears a

desperate scratching. He finds a small shovel and prepares to dig.
The end of the story is surprising, but not because of any
supernatural intervention. The narrator hears people arriving and
flees from the place, leaving the reader filled with the same
uncertainty that the narrator must always have, not knowing
whether Bieito was buried alive or not. Then too there is a perfectly
logical interpretation for those readers less prone to believe that
Bieito is the source of the noises; they may prefer to think that the
noises are figments of a hyperactive imagination, especially because
the other pallbearers seem oblivious to them. The reader is inclined
to trust the narrator, however, owing to the familiar and confidential
tone of his storytelling, addressing us as his friends and punctuating
his account with "understand me," "listen" and similar expressions
to draw our attention. This confidentiality in turn produces what
might be a deceptive sense of trust in a narrator whose account may
be nothing more—or nothing less—than a story.

"A volta" (The Return) also hints at strange or supernatural events
as the elderly widow Resenda is seen at night before her hearth. We
learn that her husband had lost his will to live when their dear son
Andresiño did not return after several years of military service in
Moorish lands. Resenda, nevertheless, continues to wait confident-
ly for many years. She hears strange footsteps approach. Could it be
an intruder? The door opens and her son appears exactly the same
as when he left home years before. Neighbors hear her singing in a
low voice, naming her son in the dead of night. The next day, when
no one answers their knocking, they break down the door of the
silent house and find Resenda lying on the floor, "her eyes so wide
open that she didn't seem dead" (24).[4]

Originally entitled "A lenda de vella Lusca" (The Legend of Old
Lusca) in the first edition, this is one of the stories which underwent
most transformation, according to the author. This intense elaboration is evident in the masterful handling of tempo and perspective.
The action is slowed down as tension mounts. As in "On the Death
of Bieito" the strange happening may be logically construed as the
hallucination of a dying woman, but the narrative point of view
registers its actual occurrence so that the reader sees exactly what
Resenda sees. In addition, the sensation of verisimilitude is
reinforced by witnesses, a passing woman and an eavesdropping
beggar. For the old woman Resenda, the townspeople, the narrator,
and the reader, the story is true and there is a distinct impression of
participating in a legend inspired by a deep-seated community of

sentiment characteristic of Galician popular folklore. Dieste's changing the title from "The Legend of Old Lusca" to "The Return," however, avoids any suggestion of romantic irony which might be present in an explicit reference to a possible legend. The impact of the ending is communicated by dividing the paragraph expected into separate sentences, each appearing as a new paragraph, for emphasis and effect.

In "Hestoria dun xoguete" (Story of a Toy) the author's imagination again assumes a collective dimension approaching popular tradition, in a tale involving strange coincidence. The sailor Bastián carves a perfectly detailed replica of his schooner as a gift for his children. When he is lost in a storm at sea, the waves take charge of bringing them the precious model with its name and port carved along the stern. The tale ends with a legendary suggestion, "Along the long white beach a woman in mourning sometimes walks, her clothes windblown, the flat basket carried on her head filled with seaweed" (35).

Several stories owe their mysterious character to the sensation of fear, such as "A luz en silenzo" (The Light in the Silence) and the aforementioned "Children's Fright." The former is recounted in the first person with a tone of confidentiality and immediacy as the narrator evokes for his listeners the first time he felt near him the "terrible empty presence of Mister Nobody" (27). He playfully minimizes the incident, however, "far from me the intention of scaring you since in any case the thing was not important." He explains that he had gone to his family's country house to straighten out some important papers left there. "I was also prone to fright," he confides; "solitude, darkness, silence, even today upset me" (28). He had left a candle lighted in the room in which he was working and went to his bedroom to get some papers. On his return the glow of the candle filling the opening of the door made him feel the presence of someone using the light, to whom he might be an intruder. Finally mustering courage to enter, he is paralyzed by fear, "in the living room, silent and somber, there was nobody" (30). As in "On the Death of Bieito," the surprise lies in the readers' disappointment at not finding anything supernatural which was what we were set up to expect. The ending is nevertheless in accord with the author's preliminary statement in his preface, "The presence of the ending should be concealed but pulsating with strong resonance in all the turns of the story" (7). After all, the narrator did say it was about Mister Nobody and confessed his propensity to fright. If we expected more, it is due to clever manipulation of imaginative suggestion on the part of the author. At the same time the story has a philosophical aspect; anticipating Heidegger and Sartre, it is a frightful confrontation with the emptiness of Being, with the experience of nothingness.

"Children's Fright" also involves recollection of a scary incident. Although the narrator recounts the story in the third person, he claims to know the dark storage cellar where the children used to play and where one day they saw a strange eye steadily fixed on them from a hole in the ceiling, as if it were the very eye of the old house spying upon them or maybe even a devil or angel. Much later, "with greater knowledge," several guesses are offered in retrospect; a cripple watching them play or an old lady who hated children, "while others, however, asserted that it all was an illusion" (70). In fact it may have been nothing more than a button dropped by a seamstress which somehow became encrusted up there. The narrator muses that now that the children are grown up, no one can say what the mysterious eye really was, but it was for them a "sort of metaphysical mirror," a first experience of uncertainty and fear. The story ends with a description of the children running out to play on the shore where the first coarse drops of rain disperse them.

There are in this tale the seeds of several childhood recollections which appear later in Dieste's *Stories and Inventions of Félix Muriel*, particularly, as we shall see, in "This Child Is Crazy" and "Juana Rial, Flowering Lemon Tree." As in the other stories we have mentioned, there are no real supernatural occurrences in "Children's Fright" that cannot be logically explained, yet who is to say that experiences produced by imagination, fear, dreams, or pure fabrication are less real for the subject (or for the reader) than others, less extraordinary? As André Breton, the father of Surrealism, pointed out, "In truth, we live our fantasies when we fantasize." [5]

II   *Tall Tales*

Some selections in the *Goblin's Archives* are what may best be described as tall tales in that they recount incredible but fascinating anecdotes. One such story is "Once mil novecentos vinte e seis" (Eleven Thousand Nine Hundred Twenty-six), exhibiting initial resemblance to "On the Death of Bieito" in that the narrator appears to have been buried alive. He tells of awakening to touch a smooth, cold ceiling, his whole body imprisoned in a metallic niche.

He realizes that he has been sleeping ten thousand years, evidently as part of a scientific experiment. He finds in his pockets a watch, thermometer, matches, tobacco pouch, pistol, flashlight, sealed letter, and a key which fits the lock so that he is able to leave the crypt. The city of Compostela has disappeared and the world seems deserted, but finally he sees a man and a child feeding on a bloody human leg hanging from a tree. An irrational horde chases after him, flinging stones and screaming in an incomprehensible tongue. Trapped between this degraded mankind on one side and the cosmic majesty of the age-old sea on the other, with tears of pity and disappointment he uses the pistol to fire warning shots, and as he prepares for the third shot, a third sharp knock at the door awakens him, "I awoke suddenly, terrified" (90). He hears the familiar sound of the milk vendor's wooden shoes which he finds consoling, yet sad and strange. As in Dieste's stories of mystery the fantastic experience can be rationally explained as a dream, but even during the height of the narrative there is a clever veiled warning when the narrator confesses that he cannot describe the crypt. "Things like that I try to remember; but the images are uncertain and not always the same. Don't put too much stock in me" (86). Here again the reader is almost persuaded to lend credence to the tall story because of the narrator's familiarity as he calls us his "friends." On the other hand, there may be nothing really fantastic about the desolate vision of the world, which in ten thousand years may quite possibly conform to the narrator's dream.

In "O neno suicida" (The Child Who Committed Suicide), a tavern keeper has just finished reading to his customers a news item about a child who shot himself in the right temple, when a vagabond who had eaten meagerly in a corner of the tavern says, "I know the story of that child." Around 1830, he explains, an old man without clothes was seen leaving a cemetery, newly born from mother earth. When still a pure spirit he had thought, "how much better to go from old age to youth than from youth to old age" (57). The Lord was intrigued by the idea and let him try it. He worked when old and became rich enough to enjoy his youth, living happily from age fifty to fifteen. At eight, however, the frightful prospect of a helpless childhood and eventual transformation into a tiny seed obsesses him to the point of desperation, alleviated by his suicide. The reaction of the listeners curiously enough corresponds to what they are drinking—the four brandy drinkers believe the tale; those with white wine are doubtful, the tavern keeper, incredulous. While they discuss it, the vagrant disappears without paying his bill, like a modern version of a minstrel who has paid by entertaining. As in the story previously discussed the narrator acknowledges certain ignorance of details. He suggests that his tale is known by others who say the hero might have loved a princess, and this allusion to other witnesses enhances its verisimilitude. The hypothetical reversal of the life process which Dieste imaginatively postulates deserves to be pondered with all the irony implicit in the anguish and afflictions of a defenseless childhood facing the prospect of disappearance.

As a curious postscript, the same inversion as that appearing in "The Child Who Committed Suicide" is present in the plots of two works published by other authors some twenty years later. The first is the well-known story "Viaje a la semilla" (Voyage to the Seed) of the Cuban writer Alejo Carpentier, first published in 1944, which follows the protagonist's life from burial to conception. Carpentier's principal interest, however, seems to lie in exploring the aesthetic effects in the rendering of such time reversal, in the strange and even humorous convolutions of the narrative which correspond to the baroque thrust of his prose. A novel by Pierre Daninos entitled *Les carnets du bon Dieu* (The Notebooks of the Good Lord), which won the Interallié Prize in 1947, follows Dieste's story in the essential points, a coincidence which the Galician writer José Luis Bugallal commented upon in *La Hoja del Lunes* of La Coruña. Dieste's own orientation is decidedly philosophical although the almost offhand way in which the story is told by the vagabond is designed to make it seem light.

Yet another twist to Dieste's basic theme may be observed in José María Gironella's short story "Miracle in the Village" in which an old man is born the same day as an infant girl. As he grows younger and she older, their ages coincide and they marry at age thirty-two. Each continues inversely until they die simultaneously, she to be buried, he to return to the maternal womb. There is much of the anguish that Dieste's story elicits, particularly in the ironic disadvantages of implacable rejuvenation, although Gironella's child's infancy is protected by the old woman. Gironella observes, for example, "It was sure, one could say with all propriety, that the boy's years 'were numbered.' An old man could live to be much older, one never knew." [6]

"O drama do cabalo de axedrez" (The Drama of the Chess Knight) is another tall tale presented in the form of a playlet, a forerunner of

Dieste's later creations in theater. It is a delightful allegorical piece recalling Calderón de la Barca's *auto sacramental* or one-act morality play *El gran teatro del mundo* (The Great Theater of Life), but instead of actors who are dissatisfied with their assigned roles, it is the chess pieces who complain of their lot in what could be called the "great chess game of life." The playlet opens with the discovery that the white knight (in Spanish, the "horse") is missing. When he does arrive, he tells the white king that he does not want to be a knight or any other piece for that matter, but rather all of them, and even the player. Other pieces complain about their assigned moves, envying others whose movements are less difficult, while the pawns emit general truths such as "later in the box we are all equal" (92) or allude to the sense of expansion of self produced by closeness to other pieces and by contact with the opposition.

One pawn recalls the experience of having travelled so many roads that "the more Pawn I was, the more I thought I alone was the whole game" (95), and another sighs, "So many roads!" Now each piece would like to be the whole game. The moon is obscured and the complaints stop with the ensuing darkness. The rook, who has been asleep, inquires about the course of the game and lights his lantern. A pawn explains that the dissatisfied white knight has gone to die at the black queen's feet. The white queen remarks how good it would be if everyone were content to be what he is, just as she is happy to be the white queen. The allegory has its humorous side in that it is quite natural for the white queen to be content with her fortunate lot since she is the most powerful piece on the board, with no restrictions on her moves. There are metaphysical implications in the white knight's aspirations, while the other pieces merely wish for the fortune of others, the knight would like to transcend the chess world and be like God.

III *People of Galicia*

A number of stories deal with different individuals and types found in a Galician sailing village, including the picturesque "Pampín" who carries his cane like a magic wand; the obedient little protagonist of the prose poem "Na morte de Estreliña" (On the Death of Estreliña), always sweet and smiling, even in death; and the little boy in "Nova York é noso" (New York Is Ours), exasperated because the other children of the village seem unimpressed by the fact that his father has just returned from New

York bearing gifts for him, to the point of claiming, "New York is ours." Some of the protagonists show an almost stubborn integrity and devotion to principle in a peculiarly Galician fashion, such as the narrator of "O caso dos tres fornos" (The Case of the Three Furnaces) who after rejecting the unfair order of the machinist to clean all of the ship's three furnaces before arriving in port, rushes to do it when another attributes his resistance to not being capable of doing it. He then leaves the ship without his pay, wanders about Marseilles, and finally hears a friendly voice in a tavern say, "I have been looking for you all day, pal." The narrator explains, "What do you expect? I returned with him aboard ship . . . The hand on my shoulder was that of my captain" (82).

Another Galician "hero" is the dying protagonist of "De cómo se condanóu o Ramires" (How Ramires Was Damned) who resists the entreaties of the priest and family, refusing last rites. "Ramires was a man who knew how to persist in his idea to the very end" (17). He had returned from twenty years in Catamarca with signs of death already on his face and with "new ideas" which disconcerted the best minds, including the priest. Only the sacristan had been able to instill in him a vague, sinister uneasiness, stating that others wiser than he had made peace with God at the hour of death. Ramires' agony evokes hallucinations, childhood memories, and tremendous anguish. Like a helpless child about to yield to the pleas of the kind old priest, he discovers the sacristan in the rear of the room with an expectant look. All his previous defiance reasserts itself irrevocably. "No and no again! The dead man's face became white, rigid as a prow. The children timidly kissed that forehead upon which the signs of the twenty years in Catamarca were marked" (19).

Another stubborn character is "O vello Moreno," (Old Man Moreno), who tells of a woman who still waits for her man to return, but in vain. Years after yielding to a traveller while her sailor husband was away—an incident which did not remain a secret for very long—the woman heard that her husband was returning and received two trunks filled with the wonderful gifts for her and the children, that he had planned for his arrival which never took place. Old Man Moreno confirms that the man was faithful and even had his wife's name tattooed on his arm. "There are people who say she loved him," Moreno continues, "but to me, to me, no one would dare say that" (43). It is perfectly obvious that the old sailor has recounted his own experience recalled from many years ago.

"O vello que quería vélo tren" (The Old Man Who Wanted to See the Train) presents another insistent Galician who convinces his daughter and son-in-law to take him to see the train before he dies. He feels sad before the "monster" that grows in size as it approaches, realizing that there are other wonders he will never be able to know, but his young grandchild is delighted and confident that when he grows up he will ride in that train.

"O vagamundo" (The Vagabond)—the protagonist in this story— emerges as an individual of a type found in every small marine village, as the narrator informs us. The girls laugh at this outcast who has never quite stopped being a carefree, wayward youth who neither attended school, tilled the soil, nor went to sea. The vagabond observes a girl with cherry lips washing clothes in the river and is ready to pounce when a shepherd's slingshot brings an apple down on his head, knocking him unconscious. He awakens to hear kissing and steals away quietly, recovering his typically detached and unconcerned pose. The story is very effective in painting the vagabond type which suddenly assumes individuality in the anecdote and elapses once more into the typical stance which marks the town vagrants in general.

There is a sort of dignity in all these Galician fellows, be they children, old men, sailors, or vagabonds, dignity and independence which they sustain in spite of the indifference or opposition of others.

IV *Nostalgia and Return*

One of the outstanding themes reiterated in *From the Goblin's Archives* is that of nostalgia for Galicia, with its corollaries of absence and return which, considering the date of publication, 1926, may reflect actual experience since Dieste had gone on a trip to Mexico in 1917 and bought his return ticket with the proceeds from a literary prize. At the same time it is surprising and perhaps prophetic that a number of the original stories of the first edition treat the theme of absence and return, "Na ponte de ferro" (On the Iron Bridge), "O grandor do mundo" (How Great the World Is), "How Ramires Was Damned," "Story of a Toy," and "The Return." Only in retrospect is it possible to appreciate the extraordinarily prophetic quality of these stories, written years before the author's emigration to Argentina, future nostalgia, and eventual return to his native Galicia after many vicissitudes and travels.

The title "On the Iron Bridge" refers to a bridge in a Gulf of

Mexico port where the narrator conversed with an emigrant whose exciting experiences made his own look pale in comparison. When asked by the narrator about the compensation he expected after a life so filled with danger and sacrifices, the emigrant confessed his secret hope to have a magazine stand, "beautifully painted, there in a little plaza I know . . . If you could see how happily the sun shines there in the morning!" (75). The narrator recalls that he was surprised then but now can appreciate and understand the emigrant's answer.

A similar sensation of nostalgia for Galicia is felt in "How great the World Is," in which the village barber travels to Buenos Aires to become rich in money and memories. Overcome by the bustling port and the interminable boulevards of the metropolis, he exclaims, "How great the world is!" After ten years abroad he returns laden with money and memories. Home again he observes the cats and hens in the streets and hears church bells and children's voices repeating an old song as they play in the rain. The familiar sights and sounds awaken in him a tender and mysterious sensation which expresses itself in the exclamation, "How great the world is!" The different forces behind the identical statement repeated in situations so dissimilar are reflected in the twofold meaning of the word *grandor*—large size and greatness in a more moving sense. While "home" may not be as large and imposing as the Argentine capital, its greatness for a homesick heart cannot be rivalled.

"De cómo veu a Rianxo unha balea" (How a Whale Came to Rianxo) recreates a "heroic" episode in the history of the author's native town recalled from the narrator's childhood. The sudden and unusual appearance of a whale which had evidently lost its way leads to a massive assault in which children, carabineers, sailors, and women participate in an atmosphere of enthusiastic animation which assumes humorous proportions. Meantime the whale, which has eluded all the attempts to capture it, turns fully around with the high tide and runs aground in the town of Vilanova, which has the privilege of getting its blubber. The narrator describes the maneuver with poetic but ironic grace, "My eyes . . . saw in the distance the brilliant spray with which the whale greeted the extension of his liberty, of his great sea" (111). Now as an adult the narrator feels a certain sadness for that poor creature who had wandered away from his element. The schoolteacher said in an article that Rianxo lost the whale owing to its lack of culture and unity, but the narrator insists that Vilanova was not superior to

Rianxo in either respect. In view of the fact that this story was written in Buenos Aires some thirty years after the first edition of *From the Goblin's Archives*, a double sense of nostalgia is evinced by the affectionate humor which accompanies the narrator's recollection of a chapter of his hometown's history and by his sympathy for the whale which could not find the "gates of his large sea" (111) and which in a sense was an unwilling emigrant unable to return to his home.

V The Art of Writing a Story

In a sort of prose poem which serves as a preface to the book, Dieste sets forth some criteria for writing stories, with particular emphasis on the ending which "must' have the virtue of making successive images simultaneous in the spirit," and must be overpowering and, though held back to the last, "pulsating with strong resonance in all the turns of the story (7). "The end," he asserts, "is an image that makes the story burst forth in the final words after being filled powerfully." This technique of working up to a powerful ending which is latent in every part of the story so that in retrospect it is not unbelievable can be observed in general and with special effectiveness in the tales of mystery, as we have previously observed. The preface also speaks of stories in terms of light, like a whirlpool circling about a lamp, but this is more than just a metaphor since in practice light appears explicitly in many stories in the form of the sun, moon, or lanterns. The presence of light in association with fantastic or extraordinary events is notable: the widow Resenda is sitting before the fire when the remarkable return of her long-lost son takes place; in "The Light in the Silence" a strange red glow is a source of fear and dread; the rook's lantern illuminates the darkness preceding the knight's demise, and the moon comes out at the end of the chess pieces' drama.

At times Dieste's fiction contains comments on the writing of stories, as in "Old Man Moreno" when the latter excuses himself for including so many details and one of his listeners adds, "With stories, one must decorate them" (41). "Yes," answers Moreno with concealed emotion since it is his own true story, "they should be decorated, very well decorated." "Un conto de reis" (A Story About Kings) is in itself a tongue-in-cheek tale about the difficulty of writing imposed as an obligation. Like other selections in the book, its characters and setting are those of a sea town, but the story itself borders on the fantastic. The narrator, requested by his newspaper editor to write a story about the Three Kings, which will appeal to young and old alike (like fish of all sizes jumping in a net, he muses), runs into a sailor in a humble tavern who expresses great admiration for his former boss Mr. Melchior. One day, he says, Melchior left the sailor as overseer in charge of a polyglot crew while he went to meet Gaspar and Balthasar in a desert. The malicious ship's interpreter fomented chaos among the seamen and the sailor's revenge was flinging a heavy sack down on him, after which he left the ship and lost Melchior's trail. He now wanders about in search of him. Just then the arrogant interpreter appears in the tavern and the sailor chases after him into the night hoping to find Melchior, as children put out their shoes for the Three Kings to fill with gifts.

The narrator returns to his office without a story. In retrospect he realizes the irony of having spoken with a sailor who served King Melchior yet having lost the opportunity to use the anecdote for his story about kings. Allusions to the actual Magi insinuate themselves into the narrative as the sailor refers to his boss as King Melchior, which surprises the narrator at the time, and speaks of the wonderful sky reader aboard his ship, an allusion to the astrological abilities of the Magi. The other two kings are mentioned by name. The frenzied search for King Melchior contrasts with the confident expectation of the children. "Without doubt there are things we never can understand" (100), muses the sailor, and the narrator agrees with him wholeheartedly. Life presents experiences which border on the marvelous but which are only accessible to those sensitive enough to discover their magic either by intuition or recollection. The ability to transcribe this type of experience into literature is one of the hallmarks of Rafael Dieste's creations.

As we have noted, *From the Goblin's Archives* forms a harmonious whole in which it is virtually impossible to distinguish earlier from later selections. There is a general sensation of remembrance from childhood or days long past. The style is relaxed as if the narrators were speaking familiarly to us across the table in a seaside tavern. In fact one of the author's favored modes of presentation is what might be called "a story about a story" in which a primary narrator meets someone who tells him a story. The result is a deepening of the illusion of reality as we listen to a narrator who in turn becomes listener for another narrator in "A Story About Kings," "Old Man Moreno," and "The Child Who Committed Suicide." In other stories, notably "The Case of the Three

Furnaces" and "On the Iron Bridge," the narrator recounts his own experiences with a tone of seriousness that makes the reader feel that he is a confidant, but in other cases such as "The Light in the Silence," "On the Death of Bieito," and "Eleven Thousand Nine Hundred Twenty-six," the narrator becomes suspect as the reader realizes that he is the victim of a clever storyteller. When the third-person narrative is used, as in "The Return," "Story of a Toy," and "Pampín," it is often to retell a story with popular or legendary flavor or to present character sketches of people of Galicia.

Throughout the book one feels more like a listener than a reader. Dieste's prose in the Galician vernacular is clear and flexible, capable of emitting brief staccato notes or of waxing poetic, reproducing sensations of humor, dread, or irony. He maintains an essential impression of simplicity, befitting the style of a sympathetic observer of humble folk. Above all he is a master storyteller who knows how to spin a good yarn which has just enough of the mysterious and unusual to ease us away from prosaic reality almost without our realizing it.

CHAPTER 3

A Galician Portrait: The Empty Window

DIESTE'S three-act play in Galician entitled *A fiestra valdeira* (The Empty Window), first published in Santiago in 1927, was highly praised by the famous American playwright Eugene O'Neill.[1] A definitive edition was published more than three decades later, in 1958, in Buenos Aires. In a conversation with Gustavo Fabra Barreiro which appeared in the literary supplement of *Informaciones* June 5, 1975, Dieste recalls the climate of those early years when he published his first works in Galician:

> To work in the language of my people has had very beneficial effects for me: It constituted a challenge to contribute to the adventure of a prose that was affirming itself and was developing at that time as a fully valid instrument of written culture.[2]

That adventure was abruptly interrupted by the Spanish Civil War but did not end either for Dieste or for a number of other Galicians of the same generation, even in exile. After his return to Rianxo in 1961, Dieste renewed the adventure with a new edition of *Dos arquivos do trasno* (From the Goblin's Archives) and was elected member of the Royal Galician Academy headquartered in La Coruña. His address to the Academy, *A vontade de estilo na fala popular* (Stylistic Motivation in Popular Speech) was published in book form in 1971 and subsequently he wrote several essays in Galician which will be treated in detail in chapter eight.

A fiestra valdeira (The Empty Window) presents the story of a portrait of Don Miguel, a former sailor who became rich in Brazil and who now entertains himself by looking through field glasses at the fishing boats visible from a window of his house. In the nearly completed portrait Don Miguel is similarly seen contemplating through a window the bay, small port, fishing boats, and nets laid out to dry—everything which reminds him of his former days. The nautical background displeases his wife and daughter who consider it an unfavorable allusion to the modest beginnings of the head of the house. They prevail upon him, after much prodding, to convince the artist to change the window for another more appropriate background, like a garden or similar view worthy of a gentleman of means.

The artist Antonio refuses to alter the painting and is supported by a group of sailors who claim the picture as their own, offering the artist a thousand pesos. Antonio wishes to give it to them as a gift. In the ensuing discussion between the sailors and Don Miguel, one of them, Garreante, brandishes a knife and with an agile and sprightly movement cuts out the piece of canvas encompassing the disputed window, which the sailors carry away amid great excitement. Don Miguel is left extremely depressed, pacing back and forth before the mutilated picture, unable to find consolation. Only at the end when Antonio, moved by Don Miguel's anguish and by the change in his family's sentiments, manages to convince the sailors to restore the window, does Don Miguel feel whole once more as he recovers his place in the community to which he always belonged in his heart, and at the same time the integrity of his own character.

I   *Individual and Community*

The essential conflict in the play is that of Don Miguel's unwilling separation from the sailing community which has in great measure formed him as an individual, for the portrait mirrors not only Don Miguel's self but also the collective soul. The community, however, is not presented in an abstract form. Each of the sailors, with the exception of the generic, anonymous old sailor and young sailor, is very clearly delineated to underscore his individuality. There is the "ragged" (according to Don Miguel's daugher) Dourado who will not accept the gift of Don Miguel's fine outfit, the blade-wielding rabble-rouser Garreante, the overly-generous sailor Caramañola, and the circumspect old school chum Mr. Baldomero.

Just as Don Miguel has his own personality, each shares the common experience of the sailing life in a different way. On contemplating the portrait even Nogueira the student sees "some memories which I thought were mine and now realize are those of a sailor" (27).[3] The picture has captured the community's past, present, and future, for even the young cabin boy Matapitos wants to be a seaman—a navigator on a big ship—and when at the end of the play the sailors speak of death, they imagine it as a happy reunion with Don Miguel as their leader on "that boat that died long ago in the fire after growing old at sea" (81) and with the Holy Child as their cabin boy. Even though Don Miguel had left the sailing life, he had remained in his home on the bay, so he cannot renounce the seascape and the community which sustain him spiritually, without losing an essential part of himself.

While the portrait in the play implies the unity or, more exactly, continuity of Don Miguel's individual integrity, it also represents another form of unity or harmony which depends on *community*, the sharing of certain experiences and a sense of common goals. Mr. Baldomeiro can see his own image in the portrait; Caramañola says it is "exactly a sky in which I want to see myself" (59); the student Nogueiras perceives common memories of the sea. The picture in effect belongs to all of them, as they claim. It is almost like a pact between them, for the community consciousness evoked in the play is much broader than that of sharing a common occupation—it is a spirit rooted in a common heritage. When the window is restored, the sailors and Don Miguel all shake hands. The sailors point out that the colors of the window are as clear and bright as when it was first painted, suggesting obviously that their friendship should be the same. Don Miguel describes the window as "yours and mine," but when the young sailor objects, Don Miguel seals the reconciliation, "I will say just ours" (80). At no moment is he resentful of the sailors' victory over him; in fact he admires their valor and their concern for him and even convinces his wife and daughter of his friends' nobility, which does not come from money but from the spirit.

II *Mirrors and Mystery*

As we shall see, mirrors are a recurring theme in Dieste's writings and appear in several related forms that in one way or another reflect reality or truth. In this sense it may be said that art forms like painting and writing mirror life. Antonio's portrait of Don Miguel has somehow achieved the marvelous by providing a mirror of his past and his deepest self, while at the same time it reflects the concrete window through which Don Miguel observes the bay. He feels something strange before Antonio's portrait of him, "I cannot judge with certainty because I have not studied or seen sufficient pictures, but I must be guided by my eyes . . . (Energetically): And not only by my eyes, for I feel something strange in front of this picture!" (30). The special virtue of this marvelous window is that others too may see themselves mirrored in it.

The mystery of the empty window and the power its absence exerts emanates from varying sources, the enigma of artistic creation and the enchantment of the sea. Don Miguel and his childhood friend Mr. Baldomero discuss art and artists early in the play. Don Miguel calls them "clever people who very tenderly trap one's being and leave it anchored forever there between the four sides of this painting" (12). Mr. Baldomero contributes a personal anecdote to show the limited power the artist has over his own creations. He once found a piece of redwood on an island and, bewitched by it, carved what he intended to be a saint but which, as if responding to the red color of the wood, turned out to be a devil whose evil influence was felt when the image was thrown into the sea.

Another allusion to the strange and unknown arises in a discussion between the artist Antonio and the student Nogueira concerning the words *urco* or *urcus*. Mr. Baldomero intervenes to describe *urco* as a very large dog which rises from the sea and howls through lanes and streets attracting other dogs. Its presence forbodes death or misfortune since *orcus* in Latin means hell. The discussion leads Mr. Baldomero to remark, "Who can know what is behind those signs and what burns behind a piece of wood one finds one day on any bank? And the same here in the beauty of this picture, who knows what is there?" (24). Everyone but Don Miguel's wife and daughter feel awe before the portrait which, as Nogueira says, "fills the house" with its marvelous light that enters through the window, the light of the sea and of remembrance.

There is yet another element of mystery, the strange way in which the play itself "mirrored" in 1927 the future of its author. It was written a full nine years before the Spanish Civil War and the subsequent emigration of Dieste, and thirty-four years before he returned to his ancestral home in Rianxo which looks out on the bay. Contrary to the experience of Don Miguel, Dieste was deprived of the real-life window while he carried another, spiritual and aesthetic, within him always. Surely the emptiness resulting from years of absence was as painful as Don Miguel's anguish before the empty window in his portrait. It is no wonder that Dieste returned to this play to prepare a definitive edition of it in 1958, three years before leaving Buenos Aires for his native Galicia.

Reality in *The Empty Window* is multiple, refractive, and like
that of mirrors reflecting mirrors. The author's observation of
Galicia's seacoast is creatively reproduced in the scene visible on
the stage, a large window through which the wharf and fishing boats
can be seen. This seascape is in turn reproduced in Antonio's
portrait of Don Miguel. Another example of multiple reality is that
of theater within theater, a constant in Dieste's plays, as later
writings prove, and in some ways comparable to the story-within-a-
story technique used in *From the Goblin's Archives*. Antonio
comments that the mutilation of the portrait is "a magnificent theme
for a play" and goes to tell it to Nogueira. "Is this a play?" asks Don
Miguel upon finding himself all alone. Disconcerted, he calls for the
cabin boy Matapitos who appears from behind the picture in such a
way that he is framed within the "empty window" from which he
says, "I am here," a note of promise and reassurance in the simple
and friendly answer which ends the second act. Later, when Don
Miguel sees Nogueira take out a notebook to write something, he
warns him that this is not a play, but Nogueira denies that Antonio
had mentioned such a thing. It seems, however, that Don Miguel is
capable of seeing himself as a character in a play, which is ironic in
view of the fact that he is exactly that. But then, on the other hand,
life itself often takes unexpected and absurd turns which are
associated with fiction and which suggest for the "actor" the strange
reality of dreams or theater.

III *Writing and Painting*

The Empty Window contains two portraits of Don Miguel, one
painted by the artist Antonio and the other by Rafael Dieste,
painted with words and, like the first portrait, intended to be
viewed by many people, for both painting and theater are visual
arts. While the painted portrait may inspire or move the imagination of the beholder, drama's movement is in itself overt, forming a
moving and speaking portrait. In this respect it is interesting to
examine how observations found in Dieste's essays on art and artists
illuminate this play with its verbal and painted portraits of the
protagonist. In his essay entitled *Colmeiro: Breve discurso acerca
de pintura con el ejemplo de un pintor* (Colmeiro: Brief Discourse
About Painting with the Example of a Painter, 1941) he intermingles the terminologies of literature and art, speaking of "plastic
language" (8), the "metrical preferences of his pictorial stanzas" (8),

and the "strong and flexible grammar of his pictures" (6).[4] He describes the effects of Colmeiro's painting in lyrical terms but explains that it is not his purpose to "put a mirror of words to all his pictures" (17).

The author points out that Colmeiro's art rests not on what looks real or verisimilitude but rather on rendering truth. He cites the artist's use of light as an example of his wisdom and maturity which can be perceived by those who know how to see this light which "becomes present in vivid and quiet reciprocity of destiny with things" (14). Instead of being used for relief, contrast, or brilliance, light is more profoundly related to interior reality and brings forth the mystery of objects. Dieste's own use of light and dark corresponds in great measure to the ideas expressed here. Don Miguel's "destiny" is paralleled by the gradual darkening of the room as the sailors enter. "It is almost night and one feels the need to light the lamp" (57).

Perhaps the greatest insight of all may be found in the author's discussion of setting in Colmeiro's paintings, for as Antonio observes in the play, without the marine background of the window his work would be a portrait of no one (51). Ironically, when the sailors come to view the portrait they claim that it is Don Miguel who no longer looks like the picture, which is his true likeness. There is no doubt in their mind about the integrity of the picture. In the essay Dieste says that Colmeiro "speaks in Galician, which is one of the honorable, loyal, and truthful ways of speaking in Spanish" (5) and that his pictures are set in places near or in Galicia. In this sense it may be said that Dieste's use of Galician as the language of the play contributes to its "integrity" in the same way that the window serves as a symbol of Don Miguel's integrity. A good translation is of course conceivable (Matilde Pomés suggested a translation into French in a letter to Dieste a year after the publication of the definitive edition), but the natural musical quality and simplicity of the vernacular enhances the harmony of the profoundly Galician characters and setting.

In his discussion of Colmeiro's use of place, Dieste states that it does not serve as background but rather as double allusion to man and earth achieved with harmony and naturality. The human figures and their natural surroundings join together in the total composition. Colmeiro, says Dieste, understands the mysterious meaning of place; "his pictures are very singular definitions of mysterious places that can't be shuffled in any way or their centers interchanged" (16).

There are places which awaken in the observer memories and deep-felt responses, "places where you were children, though you might never have been there, or where your perfect happiness begins without your knowing why" (16). These observations about place in Colmeiro may well be applied to Antonio's portrait of Don Miguel, who cannot function happily without the view of the bay which is much more than mere background. Upon observing the picture, Nogueira becomes aware of memories which he realizes are not even his because they belong to sailors, in the same manner that Colmeiro's pictures evoke memories of places one may never have seen.

Antonio's portrait of Don Miguel could well have been painted by a student of Maside, another Galician artist whom Dieste treats in a 1975 essay entitled "La estética pictórica de Carlos Maside" (The Pictorial Aesthetics of Carlos Maside) and whom he evidently considers the dean of Galician prewar painters, although Maside did not found a school as such. Maside's portraits go "like a dart, direct to the spirit, to the most intimate, unique and essential—or existential—quality of the person" (87).[5] He has a special gift for depicting the singularity of his subject and at the same time discovering the universal. This is in fact the case in Don Miguel's portrait where all the sailors can see themselves "multiplied fraternally in other faces," as Dieste says in his essay on Maside. This artist's paintings are more than just pictures; " . . . there is always behind that painting the desire to reveal something, a transpicture; and not of revealing it in allegorical form" (96). The painted window of Dieste's play is not the artist Antonio's allusion to Don Miguel's humble beginnings as his wife and daughter think but rather a vital revelation in the form of a "transpicture."

One particular reference in the essay on Maside illuminates a conversation in which Don Miguel explains to Nogueira that "the hole in the picture is for me the exit through which memories disappeared like doves and changed into twisted hawks" (71). He excuses himself for such flowery speech, suddenly recalling that his father had spoken like that when he was near death, and adds, "Death, they say, is another hole" (71). In the Maside essay Dieste twice refers to Kierkegaard's allusion to death as a hole. The first time, it is followed soon after by a metaphorical window, explaining that the artist does not judge reality but

makes it transcend in an immediate manner or he contemplates it, as Kierkegaard would say, "through the hole of death." He does not add or superimpose a transcendence. In his very abandon, in the completely quiet attitude of his look, in that gaze which renounces all judgment and likewise all classification in the moment of seeing, the window to that transcendence which covers all of us would remain as if open (88).

We have indicated earlier that community consciousness in the play is above all a spirit of common heritage. In Dieste's prologue to the Galician painter Luis Seoane's album of sketches entitled *Homenaje a la Torre de Hércules* (Tribute to the Tower of Hercules) he finds a deep-rooted sense of heritage which abounds in the artist's works. Curiously enough, the author describes Seoane in imaginative marine terms, "That big fellow you see there from behind could be the captain, but frontward, when his face can be seen, he looks more like the cabin boy" in whose pockets may be found conch shells and a marble dove that could fly.[6] Dieste admires these Galician artists (Colmeiro, Maside, and Seoane) because their pictures transcend the merely pictorial and capture the spirit of Galicia. He too has achieved the remarkable transcendence that goes far beyond the particular story of a sailor's portrait. It is easy to see why Eugene O'Neill was impressed with the play and why it was cited as the prime example of the possibility of Galicia's developing a first-rate theater in the vernacular.

CHAPTER 4
Journey, Duel, and Perdition

R AFAEL Dieste has participated actively in several aspects of the
theater, including its writing, direction, production, study,
and dissemination. His interest in writing plays evidently stems
from his Galician work *A fiestra valdeira* (The Empty Window),
published in 1927. This was followed by *Viaje y fin de don Frontán*
(Journey and End of Don Frontán), published in Santiago in 1930 by
A. Cuadrado with the cover design by the artist Maside in what José
Otero Espasandín describes as "a charming edition for its decorum
and unpretentiousness." [1]

With the advent of the Spanish Republic, Dieste became one of
the principal sponsors of the Misiones Pedagógicas (Pedagogical
Missions), founded in 1931 by Manuel Bartolomé Cossío. It
represented an unusual and outstanding effort on the part of the
Republic to bring all types of cultural experiences such as exhibits,
recitals, and theater to areas where they were never before
available. The repertoire of the Missions' theater under the
direction of Alejandro Casona consisted mainly of *pasos* (sketches or
skits) and *entremeses* (one-act farces) of Spain's primitive and
classical theater written by major authors like Cervantes, Juan del
Encina, Lope de Rueda, and Calderón de la Barca. In many
respects the unsophisticated villagers and townspeople served by
the Missions were not unlike the audiences which filled the open-air
corrales (courtyards) used as theaters in Lope de Vega's times.

Dieste was chosen by Pedro Salinas to create and direct the
Guignol (Puppet) Theater of the Missions and also to supply the
project with dramatic material based on personal invention or
popular traditions. In addition, he participated actively in all aspects
of craftsmanship—designing the little stage and fashioning the
puppets, figures, and sets, with the enthusiastic collaboration of
José Valdelomar, Ramón Gaya, Fernández Mazas, Urbano Lugrís,
and Miguel Prieto. The Guignol was incorporated into the Missions'
programs on May 15, 1932, including in its itinerary not only towns
of importance but even the most obscure little villages.

In 1934 Dieste's volume entitled *Quebranto de dōna Luparia y otras farsas* (The Breaking of Doña Luparia and Other Farces) was published by Yagüe in Madrid and the following year he received a scholarship from the Junta de Ampliación de Estudios en el Extranjero (Board of Extension Studies Abroad) to travel to France and Belgium to work on literary and staging aspects of theater. In 1936, with the outbreak of civil war, the Comisión de Trabajo Social y Cultura (Commission of Social Work and Culture) began a project of periodic festivals of theater, puppet shows, and poetry recitals, and a cooperative theater company called Nueva Escena (New Scene), directed by Dieste, began its presentations of plays written by Ramón J. Sender, Rafael Alberti, and Dieste himself ("Al amanecer") especially for the project. All of this intense cultural activity came to an abrupt end with the fall of the Republic and the exile (or as in the case of Federico García Lorca, untimely death) of the country's finest artists.

In 1945 Dieste, living in Argentina, finally yielded to his friends' requests to republish his earlier plays, since they had lost their copies with the rest of their possessions in 1939. Editorial Atlántida published *Viaje, Duelo y Perdición* (Journey, Duel, and Perdition) as a trilogy but as Otero Espasandín tells us, Dieste carried out an extensive revision and elaboration of the original works, which was not what his friends had in mind. The critic expresses his surprise before these completely new works with their already familiar characters who had grown "more mature, deeper, and more immersed in their own recesses and perplexities," and he says with all the gravity which such a statement merits that in form and expression these plays are unmatched since Spain's Golden Age.[2] In an interview with José R. Marra-López in Galicia in 1964, Dieste discussed the difficulty involved in producing plays for the stage when one is outside the "theatrical world," so he was content simply to write the works and then publish them, in view of the business problems staging would entail. He made it very clear, however, that writing plays that are also interesting reading is not in any way the same as writing "theater for reading."[3]

I Journey and End of Don Frontan

In this first play of the volume *Viaje, duelo y perdicion* (Journey, Duel, and Perdition) a Pilgrim and Don Frontán meet on an isolated road. The latter, characterizing confession as the "alleviation of

confessors," begs, "Pilgrim, have the charity to confess to the devil"
(11).[4] The Pilgrim also speaks in strange terms:

Men do not know each other or themselves and the world that shines and
that which sleeps and do not know what clarities of heaven and what
malignant turmoil everything is made of, including themselves. And
without noticing that a miracle can very well don a king's mantle or a
mended cape and even lie within the familiar that is encountered every
day, one becomes empty and stiff-necked and scorns his fellow man (12).

The Pilgrim cannot understand Don Frontán's despondent desire
for death. Asked whether he recalls his father, the Pilgrim responds
that he has a good memory and recalls plowing and eating grapes
with his father. He speaks of enigmas while Don Frontán speaks of
"labyrinths and of closed doors and of how bad a witness man is of
himself" (16). Despite the strangeness of their conversation, the two
seem to understand each other and embrace. The Pilgrim confesses
to Don Frontán how, many long years ago, his own cowardice and
repression of a charitable impulse let him be convinced by his wife
not to open his door to a supplicating voice. The following day he
found a noble old man dead in the snow with a golden light about his
head. Convinced that he had turned away "our Lord," he has
alleviated his remorse by means of pilgrimage to the Holy Land and
self-humiliation for the past fifteen years.

Don Frontán, reflecting on his own fifteen years of pride,
forgetfulness, and misery, asks the Pilgrim to look at him carefully
and then close his eyes. The Pilgrim willingly accepts the game,
showing no emotion when he opens his eyes again. But suddenly
the resemblance—for him identity itself—between the image of
Don Frontán and and that which lies in his memory becomes
evident. He removes his hat and prostrates himself, "Here I am,
Lord. Do thy will." Terrified, Don Frontán raises the Pilgrim and
takes leave, giving him his ring, "now continue on your way, for I
am going to ponder in solitude which way shall be mine" (24).

In the second scene, Don Frontán tries to evince from the
Caretaker an honest opinion of what he already knows—the
circumstances under which his father left the manor fifteen years
before. He hides in a chest to eavesdrop on a peasant couple as the
Caretaker casually inquires about the incident, but they too are
loyal and reticent. The frustrated Don Frontán suddenly rises from
the chest as if from the grave. The Caretaker sets out in the
following scene to look for Don Frontán, who has left home. The

fourth scene finds Don Frontán with some beggars at a church entrance. Most of the beggars are disturbed at his presence, not only because he takes away some of their business but also because they realize he is begging to humiliate himself. They urge him to give rather than receive and to go into the church, but with a lordly manner he cries out that if he cannot stand on his own two feet, he would rather be erased from the world.

In the next scene, at dawn before a humble inn, Don Frontán, who says he is fleeing from his shadow, meets the puppeteers Pinturillas and Salerosa. He proposes they mount a show based on his story so that their stage may be a confessional for him, and so that the audience will scorn and condemn him. Subsequently, Salerosa declares to the fun-seeking crowd at a fair that they are about to see something extraordinary. In the guignol play the Father puppet expresses hope that the Son will settle down, but the latter says he can only be a thief or a hermit. The Father can see no possible dialogue between such extremes and tries to reinforce his advice saying that he too has had to "resist the beauty of the world." He disappears and the Son pensively repeats, "Resist the beauty of the world . . . " Then the voice of Don Frontán himself cries harshly from the interior of the puppet theater, "And not make it ugly! Out!" (74). The Son disappears as if swept away by this voice.

There is a brief interval of comments from the audience. The Son reappears and then the Magician, summoned to decipher his enigmas for him, refers to the voice that the Son has recognized as his own "without feeling it pass through his throat" (75). He hints that it was the Son's future voice, "The tree speaks in its seed. The fruit in the flower. Death all the time" (75). The Son leaves as the devil tugs at the Magician. There are comments of the audience. The Son confronts a Devout Prude and rejects the heaven of which she speaks and the Magician appears with a horned Cuckold who is undecided whether he should act or not to protect his love for his wife. The Cuckold is subsequently carried in dead.

The succession of scenes is determined principally by the need for dramatic synopsis and communication of the atmosphere in order to function as the confession of Don Frontán, but it also involves the audience's comments and the intimate problems of the puppeteers Salerosa and Pinturillas, evidently moved by the spectacle. The confession of the Cuckold consulting the Magician is particularly poignant and terrifying in its brevity. Also significant, together with the humorous comments it provokes, is the confession of the Son with Tarasca ("Loose Woman") with whom "one sins and doesn't sin."

A Blind Minstrel telling of a horrible crime and the scandalous death of a cruel husband at the hands of his wife momentarily distracts the audience, whose light banter is heard in anonymous voices. On stage the Father speaks to a brightly colored rooster who announces that dawn will come but not for him. Finally the playlet assumes a sudden gravity with a decisive dialogue. The Son renounces the Father's authority asking for punishment, but the Father only blesses him, incurring the wrath of the Son who does not want to be subjected to that blessing. The Father realizes that the Son wants to be cursed to feel free. The Blind Minstrel is so impressed by the drama that he says he will abandon his stories.

The Son scorns the Father and causes him to leave. The audience protests (one woman cries out in Galician). The following scene on the puppet stage reproduces the Father's death on a cold night in which wolves roam. The public again protests when Pinturillas uses a bull for lack of a wolf. The Magician announces the presence of the Son and Don Frontán's pale face suddenly appears. The audience comments that it may very well be the Son though he looks more like an old man, in which case his own son would likewise expel him from home, for such are the turns of life. The Pilgrim suddenly appears and, on seeing Don Frontán's face, with prophetic demeanor bids all to fall on their knees to "Our Lord, the Son of Father God" before them (95).

The Puppeteers and the Caretaker speak of Don Frontán's suffering in the following scene and determine that it is best for him to return home. Don Frontán confides to the Pilgrim his intention to leave part of his estate to Salerosa, Pinturillas, and the Caretaker and the rest to him and his wife, declaring it to be a gift from his father. Salerosa offers Don Frontán the venerable doll that was the Father in the play as a souvenir, which he accepts gratefully as he prepares the trip home in the company of the Puppeteers and the Caretaker.

In the eighth scene his friends discuss Don Frontán's strange conduct, wandering about and mistreating himself in a self-made purgatory to bring upon himself humiliation as the honors he wishes for his dead father. Pinturillas analyzes Don Frontán's problem, "Another justice is missing here, the punishment which is fruitful, furious love, the anger of the father" (112). Amidst these comments the Caretaker suddenly appears, very upset because through a half-open door he has seen Don Frontán cutting away at his beard with a scissors. The latter appears, his beard badly cropped, pale and wan, and advising everyone to rest, he crosses the scene "like a ship adrift" (116). The last scene focuses upon Don Frontán who speaks to the puppet effigy of his father and finally, feeling death within him, falls to the ground. Salerosa, finding him there, laments his suffering, invoking both father and son to make peace. The Caretaker and the Caretaker's Wife mourn the loss of the "light of the manor" and "helmsman of the house."

The epilogue takes place on a radiant morning on the same road as in the first scene. Two young Peasants comment upon the disposition of Don Frontán's estate after the puppeteers left. The Pilgrim, dressed as a farmer, and his Wife come to visit Don Frontán, not knowing he has died. When the Girl they meet on the way answers their query in the past tense, "He was imposing," they realize that he is gone, leave their gifts with her, and go to the manor to take charge according to Don Frontán's wishes.

The underlying theme of the tragedy is the impossible journey of Don Frontán in search of expiation for what is tantamount to patricide. José Otero Espasandín correctly points out that Don Frontán seeks his *dies irae* or day of reckoning and within his spiritual emptiness tries to humiliate his pride "like Jonah in the whale, to be able to emerge with innocent eyes and a pure soul to enjoy the world's wonders and fraternity." [5] The critic then compares Don Frontán to Oedipus pursued by the Furies. It seems very natural to refer to Don Frontán in terms of universal myths and biblical heroes because of the grandeur of his suffering as he meets with one obstacle after another, which prevents the vituperation his soul seeks. Dieste's characters often are regional types, like this last scion of a family reared in remnants of feudalism—a feudalism never completely abandoned in Galicia—who acquire heroic dimensions by way of overt or implied mythification. It is a procedure developed further in his later fiction such as *Historias e invenciones de Félix Muriel* (Stories and Inventions of Félix Muriel).

The abundance of biblical allusions in the tragedy is especially interesting. While several grotesque scenes appear in the play, the allusions to New Testament events are not grotesque but dramatic. Don Frontán, carrying the guilt of his father's banishment and subsequent death, initates his own *via crucis*—all his wanderings in search of punishment and humiliation and particularly the three days and nights he walks about "wounding his soul with his spines

and his body with those of the woods" (97), inviting jeers and scorn.
In contrast, the journeys of the Pilgrim lead to expiation when Don
Frontán pardons him in his father's name. The Pilgrim sees in Don
Frontán an errant Christ; however he is more like a repentant
sinner, suggested by the presence of a cock in the playlet
(reminiscent of Christ's prediction that Peter would deny him three
times before the crowing of the cock). On two occasions the
repentant Don Frontán is mistaken for Christ by the Pilgrim who
had thought himself guilty of turning away Christ on that fateful
night. Like a Madonna leaning over the body of the crucified Jesus,
Salerosa laments Don Frontán's suffering and death.

The Galician setting in itself suggests an age of myths as the play
unfolds in a place in Galicia "not specifically determined, at the end
of an immature and rustic 'middle age' " and "more or less in the
past" (8). We are reminded of other biblical stories, in particular the
parable of the prodigal son, recounted in Luke XV. In the New
Testament story the younger son journeys into a far country after
taking the portion of his father's goods which he will inherit. There
he wastes his goods and his soul in riotous living. When a famine
arises and he finds himself in want, he decides to return to his
father, confess his sins, and beg to serve as a hired servant. His
father, upon seeing the prodigal son approach, feels compassion
and, falling upon his neck, kisses him and celebrates his return by
sacrificing the fatted calf. But what would have happened had the
prodigal son returned to find that his father had died because of
the suffering his son's deeds had wrought upon him? This is the
possibility Dieste explores in a Galician context with his Don
Frontán, doomed to frustration because when he is ready to repent,
his father is not there.

Condemned to seeing his father's likeness every time he looks in
the mirror or is confronted with the mirror of others' observations
and memories, he is helplessly deprived of the only possible way to
find peace in the absence of his progenitor's pardon—self-
effacement and public humiliation. His suffering makes him worthy
of forgiving the Pilgrim in his father's name, but he himself can find
no solace in a place where those he meets treat him with love and
pity rather than offering the "charity" he seeks, which ironically is
persecution and rebuke. There is further irony in the fact that the
same "freedom" from parental authority that Don Frontán had
asserted is precisely the worst punishment possible for the wayward
son who later craves the parental anger which might mitigate his

guilt. He finds that now his father's absence is much more unbearable than his presence had been to him as a youth. As Salerosa comments, he is "the most orphaned of men" (125). Neither friendship nor company can ease his existential loneliness. Don Frontán also brings to mind Calderón de la Barca's rebellious protagonist of *La vida es sueño* (Life Is a Dream), Segismundo, who wished to free himself of the fetters imposed by his father Basilio, fearful of the stars' predictions about Segismundo's ambition. Don Frontán speaks of fortune as the accident of birth which makes one man the son of another, and in a long soliloquy reminiscent of Segismundo's, he invokes the star which presided over his birth and destiny, lamenting that "dying is having been born" (120). His secret wish, which he confides to Pinturillas, would be not to have been born. Also like Segismundo, Don Frontán vacillates between the worlds of dream and wakefulness, according to stage instructions in which he "seems to dream his own acts" (9) in the scene where he eavesdrops on the peasant couple. The Caretaker later remarks about Don Frontán's appearance, "For me it was like seeing a person one thought awake and suddenly he looks at us as if he had just awakened" (32). In Calderón's play Segismundo becomes an unwitting actor in a sort of drama within the drama set up by Basilio to see how his son will behave when restored to his rightful position as prince, and it is from the errors Segismundo commits in this contrived situation that he finally learns that it pays to do good even in dreams. In Dieste's play there is also an enactment within the play which functions as a mirror of reality and though the actors are puppets, Don Frontán takes part in it, to the surprise of the audience. The similarities between Dieste's hero and Segismundo, however, only serve to obviate the contrast in the respective denouements; for Don Frontán there is no hope of reconciliation with his father or with himself.

Another literary allusion suggested by the play is Cervantes's *Don Quijote de la Mancha*. Like Don Quijote, Don Frontán begins his wandering at about the age of fifty and there are kindly people like the Caretaker and his wife who worry about him and try to get him to return home. In some respects Don Frontán may be considered a Don Quijote in reverse, because instead of taking to the road to prove himself noble and valiant like Cervantes's hero, he sets out in search of humiliation and punishment. Whereas Don Quijote's benevolent intentions meet with a good deal of frustration, he remains undaunted; Don Frontán's need for chastisement is thwarted again and again by kindly souls, submissive peasants, and the competition of other spectacles, leaving him constantly defeated.

There are echoes of the famous "Retablo de Maese Pedro" (Spectacle of Maese Pedro) from the *Quijote* in the interference of Don Frontán in the puppet show of Pinturillas. In chapter XXVI of the second part of Cervantes's novel, Don Quijote becomes so carried away by the plight of Melisendra, whom Don Gaiferos is about to rescue from a Moorish army, that he attacks and destroys the puppet theater. In Dieste's puppet show Don Frontán's voice bursts forth from behind scenes and, announced by the Magician, he appears in person. There are further implied allusions to Don Quijote when Don Frontán tortures himself for three days and nights (suggesting Don Quijote's penitence in the Sierra Morena) and when Salerosa expresses the hope that familiar faces will restore the despondent Don Frontán to normality.

Despite the fact that Don Frontán's saga is thus in some ways comparable to biblical and literary precedents, he is a unique creation whose situation is deeply rooted in his circumstance, as the only son of a just and respected father in a region where family traditions and loyalties are strongly entrenched, where the ancestral home passes from generation to generation, and the lord of the manor is the object of respect. Dieste's aforementioned indication that according to the place it could be "more or less in the past" is sufficiently ambiguous to suggest that these conditions have not changed much in some parts of Galicia. It is in this cultural context that Don Frontán's having driven his father to abandon the manor is an act which cannot easily be forgiven. After fifteen years of pride and forgetfulness he begins his journey hoping it will be as arduous and fatal as that of his father. When he speaks to the Pilgrim early in the play of "labyrinths and of closed doors and of how bad a witness man is of himself" (16), he describes in fact the course of his wanderings which lead only to closed doors of impossible expiation in a mad venture to find people who might serve as witnesses to his wrongdoing. But no one will bear witness to his blame. As the pilgrim says, "What a man deems worst in himself may be the best" (16). Everyone Don Frontán encounters insists on seeing the best in him and he remains horribly alone, for no will heap upon him the abuse he yearns for.

He is first frustrated when he eavesdrops on the Peasants who are reluctant to talk about their master and pride themselves on not having let the Caretaker wrest the secret about Don Frontán's blame from them. While the Caretaker sees his hiding in the chest as a reversion to his youthful escapades, and the Peasants view it as a ruse to catch tale bearers, Don Frontán considers it an "anticipated image of the sepulchre" (39). Scorning the frightened and submissive Peasants, he berates them for refusing him the "charity" of their curses and leaves home in a quest for punishment. Don Frontán's second attempt to humiliate himself is likewise foiled, since he cannot adequately play the role of beggar. Upon accepting material charity which he does not need, he gives it to a real beggar and ironically assumes the accustomed role of master again. When two beggars suggest that he enter the church, his reverting to the character of proud noble, insisting on doing things alone or being erased from the world, leaves the humble group shocked before an image of what seems to be the devil himself.

The sixth scene of the drama in which Don Frontán entrusts Pinturillas and Salerosa with the artistic representation of his past in order to witness his own transgressions and attract the condemnation of the crowd is one of the most extraordinary examples of the "play within a play" technique in Spanish fiction, and comparable to that of *Hamlet* with regard to the drama it generates. Technically the puppet theater serves the function of informing us about Don Frontán's youthful behavior, which is only alluded to rather vaguely in the macroplay. The reader is as eager as Don Frontán to find confirmation of his crimes, since the reticence of the Peasants in the chest scene leaves us in suspense. The microplay provides a somewhat simplified and distorted mirror of Don Frontan's sins, namely wantonness, adultery, and total disregard for moral decency. It is a mirror in which he can observe his past in a manner sufficiently detached from reality to permit him to appreciate the enormity of his acts. The grotesque elements of the puppet show, like the substitution of a bull for the wolf, reflect the grotesqueness of his real life. In fact, it becomes almost impossible to separate the two.

There are clearly two sets of actors and audiences involved. The main characters of the macroplay and we as readers or observers compose one set; the other consists of Pinturillas's puppets and the audience at the fair which expresses itself in anonymous voices. What makes the scene so unusual is that Don Frontán takes part in both. In the powerful scene in which the puppet Father implores the Son to respect love and resist the beauty of the world, the voice

of Don Frontán cries out from within the guignol, so that he
becomes an actor in the microplay alongside the puppet which
represents him, an effect which is further intensified by the sudden
appearance of Don Frontán's grotesquely pale face in the midst of
the scene of the Father's death, opening and closing his jaws in
silence before the shocked audience. The Pilgrim adds yet another
dimension to the stage presentation as he again takes Don Frontán
for Christ and calls for all to kneel before him. Pinturillas later
recognizes that there were various theaters at the same time and
that his control over his own "poor theater" was limited. And here
again Don Frontán's desire for humiliation is frustrated. The people
are distracted by announcements of freaks which vie for their
attention and the Pilgrim inspires them to reverence precisely in
the moment Don Frontán had intended to be that of his
condemnation.

In addition to the fact that Don Frontán takes part in both the
macroplay and the microplay, we as readers or audience also
participate as observers of both. While the light banter of the people
in the crowd contrasts with the dead earnestness of what is being
represented, the comments which they emit echo our own doubts
and serve as cues to how we should react. They also call our
attention to things outside the puppet show, such as Salerosa's
suffering.

The caretaker sums everything up pretty well when he comments, "here everyone loves each other and no one understands
one another" (99). How can anyone understand another when he
can hardly understand himself? It is significant that those who
befriend the distraught Don Frontán are a pilgrim, a poet, and a
woman. Through their contact with him, each comes to achieve
some measure of understanding and is profoundly changed by the
experience. The Pilgrim finds solace and a future for himself and his
wife in Don Frontán's manor. The poet, Pinturillas, is surprised and
perplexed before his own creation, by means of which he has come
to care for the real Don Frontán. The woman, Salerosa, is perhaps
the most deeply affected, not only in the guignol drama but also in
real life and in a moving soliloquy at the end of the ninth scene calls
for pity. She evokes a vision of both father and son as fighting
children in need of the mother's presence to distribute the blame
and make peace. Another note of tenderness is the little girl in the
epilogue, reminiscent of the child who in the *Poema del Cid* (The
Poem of the Cid) informs the exiled epic hero that he cannot be

helped by the townspeople because the king has threatened them with torture and death. Here too the humility of the child contrasts with the greatness of the imposing master whose death she innocently reveals to the Pilgrim and his wife simply by using the past tense.

Everyone who has come into close contact with Don Frontán is touched deeply by his drama. Outside the play others have also accompanied him on his search for impossible retribution—the reader and the author who, by implication, are profoundly changed by the experience. We may well agree with the poet and artist Pinturillas when he confesses, "We are no longer the same" (100).

II Duel of Masks

The second play of the volume, *Duelo de máscaras*, begins with a stranger's knocking at the door of Don Juan's house identifying himself only as a friend. Don Juan's cautious servant Horacio offers to chase the man away, but the master finds the mysterious personage interesting and muses that maybe it is the devil. When Horacio inquires about the visitor's name, the latter answers, "My name! My name seems to be something important! So much curiosity begins to flatter me" (146). Don Juan pretends to recognize the visitor but when Horacio leaves, we find that he really does not know him, although he is attracted by the mystery. "There is not always an opportunity to give shelter to a stranger. To waste or disdain it is almost an irreverence, an attack against I don't know what . . ." The visitor adds, ". . . against the unknown" (148). In an ambiguous dialogue the visitor seems to accuse Don Juan of being the seducer of his wife or, more exactly, of having "once taken the figure" of his wife's seducer, although he himself is her "real seducer" (153). The woman suddenly appears, explaining to her husband that she has been following him and has entered without knowing who lives there. The mysterious visitor finally identifies himself as Claudio and his wife as Rosa, reminding Don Juan of a scene they had enacted many years ago when they all were in school together. The sound of the carillon clock brings a pantomime recollection of the scene in which both Don Juan and Claudio pretended to court Rosita—Claudio eyes the young fellow, who bows to the girl. The scene disappears at the sound of the carillon again.

Evidently Claudio took Don Juan's portrayal of a bold rival

seriously and has never forgotten it. Rosa explains to her husband
that she fled from their home "to see you from afar, to remind you,
so that you would remember me, because you were forgetting me,
alienating me by trying to figure me out or discover in my soul who
knows what secret that sometimes was marvelous and other times
horrible" (161). She tells him how happy it made her to see him
seeking her because she wants to begin, to be "courted by him once
more" (161). Don Juan realizes that Claudio is still bewitched by
that fleeting moment of the past which for him was his innocent first
bow before a girl. He courteously bows before both Claudio and
Rosa now, offering them a bed to rest.

Claudio, still convinced that his wife has come to Don Juan's
house to retrieve the magic moment of the rival's courtship, refuses
to join Rosa and sets up a trap, proposing that she stay in the
bedroom alone. He challenges Don Juan, "If we meet here before
that door, one of us could die, perhaps both at the same time"
(166–67). Don Juan does not put out the light as he goes to his room.
Rosa refuses to take part in the plot and resolutely decides to flee.
To gain time, she locks the door and, taking the key with her, sneaks
out of the house, after which Horacio turns off the light. Don Juan
comes out of his room, lights the lamp again, and murmurs that "the
place of my absence should be illuminated" (171). He cannot sleep,
but after a few moments in front of the room in which Rosa
supposedly is, he resolutely returns to his room.

In the second scene Claudio, finding his wife's door closed, beats
on it, waking Don Juan. Claudio forces the door open but in the
darkness does not yet notice that Rosa is gone. Don Juan would like
to avoid a duel. "I am afraid of exceeding myself in courtesy, letting
myself be defeated or perhaps killed to spare her the pain of
widowhood" (174). Claudio interprets his concern as love for Rosa
and insists on a duel as a tribute to her. Don Juan complies; both are
mortally wounded only to find they have fought over a shadow,
since Rosa is gone. During the death scene Claudio insists that Don
Juan still hasn't recognized him, but Don Juan simply says the same
shadow will cover both. Claudio now thinks he has committed a
crime, but Don Juan absolves the dying man, who calls out to his
absent wife as Don Juan realizes how enamoured Claudio was.
The wounded master asks Horacio to finish him off, but Horacio,
convinced that he is dreaming, calls his wife to awaken him. Both
servants leave the house to seek medical help, but Don Juan expires

as he calls, "oh, Rosa! Rosa! Rosa! . . . That bow! . . . That bow is in eternity! . . . Oh, how light eternity is!" (184)

Those who have commented upon Dieste's trilogy seem to have avoided any exegesis of this particular selection, shorter in length than *Journey* and *Perdition* and a lot more perlexing, too. The ambiguity of the dialogue and the strangeness of the action leave the reader as convinced as poor Horacio that it is a dreamworld. Although the play is set in a Galician ambience, there are classical undertones in the treatment of a character whose tradition in Spanish literature is well known—Don Juan, and in the appearance of the Calderonian themes involving honor, "the great theater of life," and "life is a dream." Dreams, playacting, and masks merge in a strange, inexplicable way. The name Don Juan turns out to be a mask which obliges the man who bears it to assume the character of the seducer in another man's "dream" or imagination. Claudio, like Don Frontán in *Journey*, is imprisoned by the past, a fleeting moment barely recalled by his wife or by Don Juan, but which has embedded itself in his memory as a threat to his love. He imagines that Rosa is still nostalgic for that romantic bow offered by Don Juan and that the latter is in love with his wife. He obliges both to act out the parts he has assigned to them, to become unwitting characters in his dream inspired originally by playacting a scene of rivalry. Like Don Frontán, Claudio is tortured by an irrevocable past and cannot find peace until it is somehow resolved.

There is tremendous dramatic irony throughout the play, beginning with its subtitle *humorada* which may be translated as a whimsical piece or caprice. There is little humor in the play other than Horacio's exaggerated reactions and much more sadness in the self-imposed suffering of the jealous husband whose marriage is threatened by his desire to play a role long forgotten but which he imagines can restore excitement to the present. Claudio is the "author" of the intrigue, determined to see his suspicions substantiated. Rosa almost feels obliged to carry out her role and Don Juan finds himself in the middle, forced to assume the Don Juan mask he had worn innocently many years before. He understands what is happening insofar as it is possible to make sense of the events:

Is he [Claudio] crazy? Are both crazy, he and she? Perhaps they are looking for each other and cannot find each other and have come to seek one another here, at the home of the supposed seducer, in a supposed risk! (169)

Don Juan recalls that his gesture was simply part of a game in which he played a theatrical rival while Claudio, who was even then in love with Rosa, took his rivalry as the truth. After so many years Claudio insists that the play, interrupted long ago, continue, complete with a test of the lady's will to determine her preference, and a duel as a final tribute. Ironically, Claudio has awakened feelings not intended in the original innocence of the act. Yet Claudio is fully aware of the fact that he too is playing a role. "It is so easy to play my role better than myself" (154). When he expresses his hatred of Don Juan, the latter answers that he is only playing his role. The dialogue between them in the first part of the play is filled with ambiguity:

Don Juan: I see your mask!
Visitor: That which you give me . . . Now you don't see me; you are neither
    my friend nor my enemy; you don't know me nor am I important to you.
Don Juan: Your mask and mine! Do you see mine? I envy you! No mirror
    has been able to offer that spectacle to me yet.
Visitor: You have no profound fear toward anyone . . .
Don Juan: Yes, yes, I think you see it since you are speaking with it and
    make me feel that it is mine. And here indeed my profound fear can
    commence.
Visitor: Fear of nothing, of no one, since nobody exists for you. Not even
    you yourself, I think.
Don Juan: What a fine occasion to know me if I did not suspect that you are
    painting upon my stupefied face the portrait of another!
Visitor: Of whom?
Don Juan: Of the seducer of your wife. I mean, of the one who plays you
    (156–57).

This rather Surrealist dialogue seems to suggest that Don Juan is really the ideal mirror image of the tortured husband, as the eternal suitor, almost as if his presence were necessary to confer upon the marriage the mystery and challenge which have dissipated with time. Rosa, called upon to carry out the role of suspected wife, gives the following appraisal of the situation:

It almost seems that he wants to confirm his fears, to have proof that the mortal fear of his heart is not unfounded, to make me see the falseness of mine, and to aggrandize himself horribly in his misfortune, like a friend of the gods, like a diver into dreams, like a diviner, by opening a pit, a great mystery in which I must jump in order for the two of us to feel unfortunate, to cling to each other like never before in a shipwreck, in the terrible truth. No, no, no, I don't want it! (169–70).

Claudio also realizes the great attraction of mystery as he asks, "In what mystery of those two do I want to penetrate? What am I in love with: her or that mystery? Well, it's all the same. I want to kill them" (172). None of the characters can resist the fascination of mystery: Don Juan feels compelled to open his door to the unknown visitor, Rosa cannot refrain from her wanderings, and Claudio cannot stop pursuing the image of Don Juan. All have been playing roles in a nightmare which draws into it all those present, even the bystander Horacio, whom Don Juan tells that he has just entered a dream. Horacio calls out to his wife to tell her that he is imprisoned in a nightmare and after she strikes his face to awaken him, he still is not sure whether he is awake or dreaming.

Don Juan is first one who suggests the idea that everyone is dreaming. "All this is nothing but a bad dream and as the height of friendship, we three are dreaming it at the same time, even though each one does it in his own way" (165), but he invites his guests to rest, seeing no need to prolong a bad dream deliberately. Don Juan warns the others, "You will be surprised and I think you will even laugh at this strange dialogue if it can be recalled in the light of day" (165). Claudio insists on continuing the dream until he knows how it ends; only then can he feel that things will be clear on waking. Don Juan explains that perhaps it was necessary for them to dream this in order to repair some involuntary injustice which might have disturbed the infantile grace of what was originally a game of rivalry. There is little difference in the play between dreams, plays, and real life as everything seems to take on the confusing, ambiguous, unexplainable character of a dreamworld.

As is frequent in Dieste's writings, marine terminology and background are important in the play. The word "shipwreck" acquires metaphorical implications in Rosa's conjectures that among other possibilities, Claudio unconsciously wishes to provoke the misfortune of both so that they will cling to each other in the shipwreck with more love than ever. Don Juan's parlor is amply described in the stage directions as having windows which illuminate the outside like a lighthouse lamp, appropriate in view of the fact that the couple seems lost and seeks the solution there. Other stage directions have imaginative suggestions. The parlor has

an iron lantern which oscillates so that the shadows emitted bring to
mind the masts of a ship in which Don Juan seems as "illustrious
passenger" and Horacio, the captain. For Don Juan dawn brings the
image of shining waves (180) and he tells Claudio and Rosa that they
will awaken from the bad dream to see the ocean the next day, leave
their footprints on the beach, and hear gulls shriek (165). At a
crucial moment, when Don Juan decides to return to his room
rather than enter Rosa's, the chant of a sailor returning to his ship in
the early dawn is heard (169).

The marine lantern is almost as important as the cherry-colored
lamp which is an element of marvel in *Historias e invenciones de
Felix Muriel* (Stories and Inventions of Félix Muriel). Don Juan
insists on illuminating the place where he is absent, but Claudio is
fascinated by darkness, savoring the mystery which inspires him to
exclaim upon breaking down Rosa's door, "what wonderful darkness" (173). Don Juan tries to keep the light lit, but Horacio turns it
off. Again his master comes into the center hall to turn on the light.
At the end Horacio attempts to put it out as Don Juan expires, so
ironically the latter's desire to illuminate "the place of his absence"
results in illuminating that of his final and irrevocable absence,
death. "Who knows!" he ponders in the final moments of the play.
"If you had let me put it out . . ." (182). The carillon clock also
assumes the force of a symbol as its sounds move us to the past and
then again to the present, and Rosa extends her hand to touch it
without reaching it.

There is a certain perverseness and fatality in *Duel* which is
reminiscent of Valle-Inclán, although our author's treatment of love
is much more delicate than that of his countryman. Claudio, like
Don Frontán, is author of his own misery. "Everything which in
some way resembles happiness is always so insecure" (159), he
asserts at the beginning of the play. Generally it would seem that
happiness is threatened more by what the future may hold than by
some forgotten event of the past, but Claudio rather perversely is
intent upon resurrecting a moment which he feels threatens his
happiness. All he succeeds in doing is driving his wife away and
awakening in Don Juan memories of an innocent gesture long
forgotten.

Claudio's insistence on testing his wife recalls the figure of
Anselmo in the novelette by Cervantes entitled "El curioso
impertinente" (The Impertinent Curiosity-seeker), included in the
Quijote, who convinces his best friend to test his wife's fidelity, with

fateful results. While in the *Quijote*, the story is told in a realistic way, in Dieste's play the atmosphere is dreamlike, with emphasis on mystery and absurdity. The characters act out their parts in accordance with the masks they have donned either by their own volition or by imposition of others.

The theme of the suspicious husband is as old as Spanish theater, yet Claudio represents a departure from the usual image of the husband concerned for his honor since he is jealous of a memory, which is absurd since even an infidelity of desire previous to marriage would not threaten his present status. Don Juan is the part of Claudio he himself would like to be, the mask he would like to wear—that of the perennial lover. Don Juan hints at this in conversation with Claudio, insinuating that he has no real identity except what the other sees in him as a mask.

In this respect, Dieste's play reminds us of the last part of Federico García Lorca's play *Amor de don Perlimplín con Belisa en su jardín* (Love of Don Perlimplín and Belisa in His Garden), which was written about the same time as *Duel* and was completely unknown to our author. In Lorca's farce the old bachelor Don Perlimplín marries his young and seductive neighbor Belisa and assumes the identity of a secret love to fulfill his romantic wife's need for a young love and for mystery. Don Perlimplín acts out the role of the rival he has invented and kills himself. As we have seen, Claudio invents a rival filled with the mystique generated by Don Juan, man and myth, resulting in the death of both. Despite substantial differences between both works, there are a few striking similarities. In his excellent edition of Lorca's play, E. F. Granell notes that a childhood memory, the story of a woman who strangled her husband, discouraged Don Perlimplín from love. When he finally decides to marry, he invents the comedy of a young lover "in order to cure the flirtations and not the infidelity of his wife and to free himself from the 'dark nightmare' that tortures him." [6] In both plays a childhood memory and an infidelity that does not really exist are involved and there is a desire to endow married love with mystery, with fatal effects. These similarities, however, are the results of pure coincidence in two dramatists with an innate feeling for portraying the human craving for impossible fulfillment in dramatic terms fraught with Surrealist wonder and strangeness.

It is interesting to observe the changes Dieste introduced with respect to the play's first version included in the volume *Quebranto de doña Luparia y otras farsas* (The Breaking of doña Luparia and

Other Farces) in 1934, in which the titular masks appear explicitly as such. In one scene two masks, caricatures of Don Juan and Amadís (a famous fictitious knight whose exploits inspired Don Quijote), duel furiously with clubs and, at the close of the farce, two masks of delirium insult each other and finally fall on the bodies of Don Juan and Claudio. Don Juan's character is rather superficial and harsh in that he is annoyed by Claudio's presence and stays away from Rosa's room simply to avoid the "inconvenience" of having to kill Claudio in his house. The new version adds a poetical atmosphere related to the use of light, enhances the background, provides the dimension of another perspective with Horacio and his wife, and makes Don Juan much more human and sensitive behind the mask of seducer which his name, reputation, and Claudio's imagination have imposed upon him.

III   The Perdition of Doña Luparia

The opening scene of the third play in the book, *La perdición de doña Luparia* finds Doña Luparia on her way to the city with Rocío, an orphan whom she intends to pass off as her ward kidnapped in infancy by gypsies and now being returned to her illustrious parents, thanks to Doña Luparia's good offices. On their journey they stay at the guest house of some comfortable farmers, Silvia and Pablo, whose son falls in love with Rocío. Neither the young man's parents nor Doña Luparia are happy about this romance, but when the latter tells her made-up story to Silvia, the mother is relieved to learn about Rocío's respectable background and offers her guardian six ounces of gold to convince Rocío's parents to look favorably on the marriage. The next night, when Rocío is supposed to run away with Sergio in secret, Doña Luparia spirits her away. Pablo authorizes his son to go after his love but warns him that if he returns without her, he will be shot.

Rocío meantime realizes that Doña Luparia is a witch and a go-between who says she "trots" for others, having suffered in love herself because of innocence. In the city Doña Luparia sets up old Don Serafín as a masked suitor, but two libertines show up unexpectedly at the same time. Don Serafín, defending Rocío from the advances of one of them, is killed by him. Sergio fortunately appears at the door and the lovers flee.

Back at the farm Silvia tries to avoid disaster by selling her husband's shotgun to a Guest housed there. A travelling Guitarrist tells Pablo of having seen the lovers going in that same direction and the Guest has seen them in the orchard. Sergio and Rocío are fearful of parental rejection, but there is a happy reunion and they prepare for the wedding as the Guest, to everyone's surprise and delight, offers a gift of six ounces of gold. The plot seems resolved, but then Doña Luparia appears there to blackmail the lovers and the parents for Sergio's possible implication in Don Serafín's death. Silvia offers as a gift the six gold coins, but after some reflection, Doña Luparia declines.

The Guest, in whom Rocío sees a sponsor, intervenes calling for a mirror to confirm what he has observed—that Doña Luparia is really touched by the lovers. He leads her to come to grips with her own misery, awakening in her the desire to serve as sponsor for the wedding, since the go-between has unwittingly contributed to the flowering of true love. This revelation becomes clear to her upon following the Guest's exhortation to look at herself in the mirror held by the lovers. Upon seeing her image between them, she begs to be the bridesmaid, a request which Sergio's father allows the Guest to answer. His peremptory yet fraternal no frightens the lovers, who drop the mirror. Doña Luparia manages to say thank you, bow before these people who are as defenseless as she and, covering her face with her hands, disappears, as broken as the pieces of the mirror that lie on the ground. Silvia feels compassion for the departed Doña Luparia and laments the fact that "we know nothing" and that love has its price. The Guest leaves for his home accompanied by the Guitarrist and his young wife Aurora as the lovers see them off.

The first version of the play, originally called *Quebranto de doña Luparia* (The Breaking of Doña Luparia), published eleven years earlier, in 1934, is about half the length of *Perdition* and ends with the arrival of Sergio and his rescue of Rocío in the city. Doña Luparia, in Don Serafín's mask, disappears and Rocío explains that the witch's powers have been rendered impotent by Sergio's presence. The new version contains additional characters such as the Guest, the Guitarrist, and Aurora who provide lyrical effects and the elements of friendship and mystery. The character of Doña Luparia is greatly enriched. At the end of *The Breaking of Doña Luparia*, Rocío conjectures that the witch probably escaped through the chimney on her broom, but realizes that without Doña Luparia she would never have had the opportunity to meet Sergio. This last observation is developed in the new version in which Doña Luparia is permitted to become aware of the part she has played in the lovers' happiness. Thus she discovers that reserve of goodness that had lain hidden within her, which now has been tapped by Rocío and Sergio. The decidedly fairy tale ending of the early play is changed with the addition of all the events which lead to the internal apotheosis of Doña Luparia resulting in the "perdition" of her witchlike nature.

The play seems to examine the uncertain and variable nature of truth and pretense. We do not know when we are pretending and what our real nature is, so it is not surprising that we understand even less the actions of others. Silvia's words at the close of the play reiterate this theme, "we know nothing" and "everything is going to seem like a dream" (333). There are numerous disguises, some donned voluntarily, others assumed unwittingly. Many characters are themselves surprised to find their roles changed and are perplexed by their own words and actions. What we are and what we seem are determined in part by our intentions but also by the way in which others view us. In this sense people mirror each other, but not always faithfully.

Sometimes a brief glance may reveal a momentary truth which has lain hidden beneath masks, disguises, and lies which do not allow our innermost being to be discovered. Like magicians surprised at their magic, Dieste's characters view life with perpetual wonder toward others' actions and their own. Strange emotional outbursts of anguish, compassion, or happiness depend on fragile circumstances subject to chance and coincidence. It would seem that true love and friendship are the only means of attaining some degree of understanding of self and others, to the extent that this is possible in a world in which people cannot comprehend their roles imposed by an uncertain destiny which is life's deepest mystery.

Silvia thinks that her husband is capable of carrying out his threat to kill their son if he does not return with Rocío, but we can see, given Pablo's character, what measure of pretense there is in his threat. Rocío is surprised to see the Doña Luparia she regarded and trusted as a respectable townswoman turned into a conniving exploiter. A change in role in several characters brings them to a sort of apotheosis, as in Don Serafín, the ridiculous, enamoured old man who turns out to be Rocío's protector, a role which proves fatal. The Guest finds himself assuming the role of sponsor, judge, and mediator. The greatest apotheosis, however, is that of Doña Luparia, in the perdition of the witch and the emergence of the woman. Confronted with the mirrored image the Guest has discovered in her, she turns from exploiter and blackmailer of the lovers to their protector. Thanks to the Guest's intervention, she realizes her evil intent has yielded something beautiful and is able to appreciate the value of true love, clear her heart of rancor, and see the lovers as a renewed Adam and Eve.

Thus we see that many of life's ironies rest on chance, for Doña Luparia's designs are responsible for bringing the lovers together, and even her invented story about Rocío's past contributes to the mystery Sergio finds fascinating in the girl. The Guest characterizes Doña Luparia no longer as "chance, the creditor with the face of an old woman, but grateful chance, with a face of surprise" (324). Indeed, no one seems more astonished at her unforeseen role than Doña Luparia herself, as she takes off, perhaps to consummate her redemption with further wandering and reflection. She has come a long way to learn about herself. As she says in the very first scene, "One must travel far in order to see. Even to see what is before one's eyes" (187).

Echoing the fact that principal characters such as Doña Luparia and Don Serafín are not what they seem, the wandering Guitarrist who stops by the farm pretends to be blind so that others will imitate him and thus listen more attentively to his music. His disguise is also symbolic, "I disguise myself as a blind man because I know I am blind" (274). For Pablo, the Guitarrist has another role, that of angelic messenger who informs him of the lovers' arrival. Reality, then, is not a simple matter since it depends a good deal on chance and circumstances which we are too blind to see clearly and understand.

Underscoring the variable nature of roles imposed by destiny are such symbolic elements as masks, mirrors, dreams, disguises, lies, and playacting. All are means of falsifying reality in some way. Doña Luparia invents a "novel" in which Rocío is being returned to her parents. Don Serafín masks his age hoping that Doña Luparia's "surgeon" (himself a disguised servant) will alter his face into a more permanent mask. Rocío and Sergio playact, feigning extreme courtesy in response to the indignation his mother and Doña Luparia exhibit at their familiarity. Rocío confesses to Sergio when she frees herself of the lie in which Doña Luparia had her imprisoned, "I myself don't know me. I think I am dreaming. Oh, if I awoke and it turned out that you were the only truth of the dream" (218). Doña Luparia defends the need for disguises, explaining that

it was once a practice of princes but that humble people are even
more in need of disguises to walk the earth:

But now comes the greatest teaching. He who plays a part, though it be
fleeting, undertakes certain obligations. The emperor who acts like a beggar
at the door of a cathedral cannot refuse the coin left in the palm of his hand
(319).

(We are reminded of Don Frontán's experience in the first play of
the volume.) She feels she was playing a part with Doña Silvia and
thus her intentions in accepting money to favor her interests were in
good faith. Rocío is largely a product of her fantasies and the trip was
forged by her dreams.

The mirror, a constant in Dieste's works, is used to show that we
are not always aware of the roles we are playing. The Guitarrist's
wife Aurora notes that "it is dangerous to play with mirrors," but her
husband adds that it is "more dangerous to play the part of a mirror"
(326). All who judge others and their motives may be defective
mirrors, for even good ones reflect reality in reverse. Good and
pious intentions, however, are capable of discovering the truth—
Pablo knows the Guitarrist can see, Sergio falls in love with Rocío
despite the false pretenses, Rocío feels instinctively that the Guest
is their best man, and the Guest knows there is good in Doña
Luparia. It is altogether fitting that the Guest's name is Don Pío,
meaning Pious. Others have seen Doña Luparia differently. Rocío,
who initially allows herself to be a part of Doña Luparia's fantasies,
later says, "I am seeing your skull!" (228), and is frightened at
finding herself in her strange company.

Toward the end of the play Doña Luparia considers all her powers
useless, her own words senseless. She fears that she cannot trust
even those words that come from the depths of her soul, "I want to
say thank you, but I want to say it truly, and still cannot, sir, I still
cannot." "Help," she begs, "for my word which I do not
understand!" (331)

One critic refers to the sensation of "perennial miracle" that the
play calls forth, citing the Guest's comment that "antiquity is born
every day with the sun." [7] This is evident in the freshness with
which the Adam and Eve myth is viewed in the enamored couple.
In this respect the name Rocío, meaning dew, is symbolic,
especially when accompanied by that of the Guitarrist's wife Aurora,
dawn. There are other concepts revitalized in the play that occur in

Spanish classical literature, for Don Serafín is a variation of the traditional, enamored old man and Doña Luparia an echo of Fernando de Rojas's great Celestina. Her allusion to "trotting" also evokes Rojas's model, the Archpriest of Hita's famous *Trotaconventos* or Convent-Trotter (mediator or go-between of lovers). J. Otero Espasandín refers to the best of Golden Age theater when judging the importance of Dieste's plays.[8] It is not surprising that this comparison comes to mind, for *The Perdition of Doña Luparia*, while revealing the mysterious quality associated with Galician literature, recalls the classical Spanish theater's penchant for disguised travellers, duels, and storybook romances. As the Guitarrist notes at the end: "There are still weddings as in olden times!" (335) "And roads," adds Sergio. This prompts the Guest's statement about antiquity's daily rebirth, for he says even he feels ancient. His role in the play, in fact, recalls that of the kings who resolved problems in Lope de Vega's plays. In conclusion, it should be noted that Dieste himself returns to the theme of the witch as human being in 1943 with his story "Juana Rial, Flowering Lemon Tree" in *Stories and Inventions of Félix Muriel*.

IV   Journey, Duel, and Perdition *as a Trilogy*

Dieste's decision to join these three revisions of earlier plays in a single volume suggests the presence of some common incentives and inspirations. An unsigned review published in *La Nación* of Buenos Aires on May 12, 1946 speaks of "the unity of Mr. Dieste's book, unity created and sustained by the notable spirit of a strong caste of souls and voices," evidently alluding to its Galician characters. In spite of the divergent designations of the works as tragedy, caprice, and comedy, the three plays reveal persistent ideas and motifs present in Dieste's later writings.

First of all, it is significant that all three evolved from earlier versions of much shorter length. The correspondence between Rafael Dieste and his brother Eduardo shortly after the publication of *Journey and End of Don Frontán* in 1930 sheds some light on the process of elaboration. While Eduardo found the original play strong, classical, and sober, he observes, "Your defect and mine (*El viejo* [The Old Man]), I think, is brevity . . . Yes, I understand . . . The line of simple groupings is so pure and noble."[9] He suggests that many a succinct comment in the play could easily inspire beautiful speeches and likens the effect of schematic dialogue to that which the perplexed and stupefied peasant woman experiences when Don Frontán leaves the chest where he has been hiding and places a pumpkin in her hands. As for the possibilities for further development of the central character, he speaks of longitudinal extension (adding episodes) or thematic extension (intertwining other themes with the dominant one, as Shakespeare does), although he finds *Journey* excellent as it stands, inviting the audience's participation by leaving the pumpkin in their hands.

The author's reply (January 3, 1931) states that he finds the "line of simple groupings" not only pure and noble but very tragic. He expresses his preference for extending the work with variations on the theme resulting from essential links between the episodic material and the dominant theme. He also speaks of his intentions to write "another farce about the last days of Doña Luparia" and perhaps even another about Salerosa and Pinturillas. "With the one already written, it would make three, classical number in the theater." In the final consideration he adds that any plot can be turned into true and substantive art if it is humanized and subjected to the rigor of a poematic line.

Surely all these considerations entered into the later reworking of the plays which, while not exactly the three Dieste had originally contemplated in order to arrive at the classical number in the theater, did produce the volume *Journey, Duel and Perdition*. The mature versions reveal a combination of longitudinal extension (particularly in the case of Doña Luparia) and of episodic variations. Other additions softened abrupt transitions, lengthened dialogues, and further humanized characters, all of which make the works less difficult than Eduardo had feared the audience or reader might find in the rapid phrase and classical simplicity of his brother's first writing. One of the most surprising aspects shared by all three plays in the volume is that they involve journeys of one sort or another. The motives for travel differ—for Don Frontán it is an obsessive attempt to accumulate humiliation and punishment, for Claudio it is an equally obsessive quest for reparation and certainty, for Doña Luparia it is promise of fortune and gain. Her words capture the essence of Dieste's journeying protagonists, "One must travel far in order to see. Even to see what is before one's eyes" (187).

Don Frontán's journey, motivated by a desire for atonement, is linked to a peculiarly Galician tradition dating from earliest times, that of transversing the Camino de Santiago or Saint James's Way to his shrine at Santiago de Compostela in La Coruña, reputed burial place of the apostle who was the patron saint of Christian Spain's seven-century struggle against the Moors. In medieval times Saint James's Way was filled with pilgrims, particularly from France, and it was common to see minstrels and entertainers like Aurora and the Guitarrist of *Perdition* and Salerosa and Pinturillas of *Journey* along the route. The peripatetic nature of so many of Dieste's characters, not only in the trilogy but also in previous and subsequent fiction, recalls this archaic tradition in a region still governed by customs and a way of life rooted in the past, in a "middle age" that "according to the place, can be more or less in the past" (8), like the setting of *Journey*.

The constant travelling we find in the trilogy also reflects the author's own journeys as a travelling author, stage manager, and puppeteer with the Pedagogical Missions in the early 1930's for rather ingenuous audiences much like the fair goers entertained by Pinturillas and Salerosa. And if the reader thinks that it is too coincidental that Rocío should find true love quite accidentally when Doña Luparia stays overnight at Sergio's parents' farm, it may be pointed out that Dieste himself met Carmen Muñoz in Cáceres, one of the places on the tour of his guignol theater and they were married soon after.[10] The structure of Dieste's plays often suggests journeys of unforeseeable destinations. Recalling his improvisation of plots for his puppet shows, it seems almost as if the plays had written themselves, as they meander into sometimes unrelated ruminations or unexpected complications reminiscent of dreams. In *Perdition*, for example, just when one thinks the plot is resolved with the return of the lovers and the reunion with Sergio's parents, Doña Luparia appears to provide yet another problem.

Since the original versions of the three plays date from 1930 and 1934, their wandering characters may be viewed in retrospect as a prophetic foreshadowing of the writer's personal destiny, as we have noted with reference to his stories in Galician, with an irony as dramatic as any that appears in his plays. It is not difficult to imagine that Dieste must have perceived this irony as he prepared to reedit the trilogy for Editorial Atlántida in Buenos Aires a decade after the Spanish Civil War had launched him on an odyssey far from his Galician shores.

Strange quirks of fate are observed again and again in Dieste's plays (a beggar in *Journey* remarks, "One always ends up seeing what he didn't believe" [40]), but what is characterized as unlikely in art may well occur in real life. Perhaps it is for this reason that

reality in the trilogy has a distinctly dreamlike quality. Both Don
Juan and Rocío have the sensation of participating in a bad dream,
while Don Frontán acts as if in a dream. One has the impression
that Dieste shares with Calderón de la Barca the feeling that life
may be equated with dreams. An air of mystery marks events,
dialogues, and people. Salerosa laments in *Journey*, "Everything I
thought well known turns into ignorance" (126); Don Juan muses, "I
myself begin not to know what my words mean" (164); Silvia
concludes in *Perdition*, "We know nothing" (333). Each character
could well repeat with Doña Luparia, "I have a treasury of secrets"
(320), secrets of which he or she may not even be aware.

Among the characters in these plays, there are some with a
profound capacity for understanding others. The Guest, for
example, has confidence in the depths of being and the secret
sources from which "conversion" may spring. Even Doña Luparia is
wise, though it be in deceit, with regard to the motives and
behavior of others. There is a certain amount of Machiavellianism in
her, as in real life people, but at the hour of truth, it is swept away
by her before the truth or it is the agent of its own undoing. Both
Don Frontán's and Doña Luparia's refractory spirits are subdued,
by different means and circumstances. Each is a complex mixture of
good and bad which eludes any attempt at simplistic characterization or the passing of an irrevocable verdict. When the Pilgrim
speaks to Don Frontán of men's ignorance of one another and their
lack of knowledge of "the world that shines and that which sleeps"
(11), he alludes to the reverent suspension of judgment before the
secret profoundness of human beings and the coincidental way in
which their destinies may cross. This type of intuition is found in all
three plays, in different situations and perspectives, and contributes
to the impression that they form a trilogy, although the author has
never expressly called them that.

Mystery and uncertainty attract many of Dieste's characters,
providing motives for perplexity on the part of these characters as
well as the reader. The dialogues demand a good deal of
concentration, for they are filled with mysterious allusions not easily
deciphered by the listener. This mystery extends beyond the
framework of the play itself so that the reader begins to feel caught
up in the invention just as many characters find themselves taking
part in the fantasies of others—Don Frontán as an actor in the
guignol playlet he asked Pinturillas to create, Don Juan in the role
of seducer that Claudio has forced upon him, and Rocío subjected

for a while to Doña Luparia's plans for her. As in dreams, people find themselves playing unexpected parts imposed by circumstance or by accident. Another quality which contributes to a dreamlike atmosphere, and more exactly to that of a nightmare, is the obsessive nature of characters like Don Frontán, Claudio, and Doña Luparia, bent on carrying out their plans to the point of self-effacement.

The repeated presence of mirrors suggests another mode of representing reality for, like dreams, plays, and fantasy, mirrors reflect life. Don Frontán's father sees himself as an annoying mirror for his son and the latter finds in his own mirrored face the inescapable image of his father, but the playlet also serves as a mirror in which he can observe his past. The Guest's mirror in *Perdition* reveals to Doña Luparia an image of herself which is surprising, and Claudio's memory in *Duel* functions as a mirror of an irrevocable moment of the past.

Another common element in all three plays is that of implied allusion or mythification of the characters, a tendency increasingly cultivated in later works. José Otero Espandín compares Dieste's language in the three works to that of the great writers of the Golden Age, Calderón, Quevedo, Góngora, and Gracián. It may be added that his characters also spring from Spanish classical traditions. In Don Frontán there are echoes of Don Quijote and Segismundo; Don Juan inherits a centuries-old reputation for being the master seducer; Doña Luparia is Dieste's version of Celestina. Nevertheless, these characters familiarly rooted in classical works surprise us with the irony of their destinies, as Don Frontán becomes a frustrated Segismundo who cannot make peace with his father or find the mistreatment which so easily befell Don Quijote, Don Juan a reluctant version of his namesake, and the "infernal go-between" Luparia the unexpected benefactor of true love. An accompaniment of other characters seemingly lifted from Golden Age theater, including blind singers, minstrels, puppeteers, faithful servants, and humble peasants, enhances the archaic quality already implied in the major characters.

There is yet another matter which remains to be dealt with in *Journey, Duel, and Perdition,* and that is the relationship of Dieste's theater to that of his famous countryman of the Generation of 98, Ramón del Valle-Inclán, to whom he has been compared by several critics.[11] Both authors were born in maritime villages of Galicia, travelled to Mexico early in their careers, and were active not only in writing theater but also in staging it. They display similar attitudes toward their craft in that they are committed to aesthetic values involving intense elaboration of the raw materials of reality with particular preference for fantasy, legend, and the use of farce, generally in Galician settings. Both evince a wish to give theater a certain dignity as art, freeing it from the intentions of realistic documentation and raising it above the commonplace (something which may be achieved by the farce, which interposes sufficient distance between the reader or observer and the representation so that he is moved intellectually as well as emotionally by the spectacle). With allowances for individual differences, such as Valle-Inclán's modernistic prose, their plays exhibit careful attention to language and dramatic structure. Dieste is particularly wont to nurture suspense and mystery by withholding information and cultivating ambiguity. Like Valle-Inclán, he is not an "easy" author; one must delve into their dramas to discover what may lie half-hidden and inconspicuous in the dark corners of the paradoxical and the absurd.

There are, however, a number of essential differences which give Dieste's work a character quite distinct from that of Valle-Inclán's literary production. Juan Gil-Albert points out a few of these:

Valle-Inclanesque stories seem to resound in this Galician poet, but the language spoken by Dieste's figures is less sonorous and their mannerisms less gesticulating, their melody more one of thought than of aesthetic and spectacular action.[12]

Valle-Inclán, then, approaches melodrama, while Dieste removes his farces from everyday reality only far enough to make them seem more like dreams, in which coincidence is not startling and escape is impossible. As for Valle-Inclánesque fabrication, the impression of similarity may be somewhat deceptive. The older playwright generally portrays the absurdity of man's being in plots involving corruption, incest, revenge, eroticism, and blasphemy. His *Comedias bárbaras* (barbaric plays), for example, set in Salnés in Galicia, pose a negative view of traditions and superstitions in an oppressive, medieval, and pagan atmosphere. In *Cara de Plata* (Silver Face) the Galician lord of a degenerating lineage, Don Juan Manuel Montenegro scandalizes his son Silver Face, in contrast to Dieste's *Journey and End of Don Frontán*, in which the son is the sinner.

Valle-Inclan's characters display avarice, lust, baseness, sensuality, and a demoniacal nature. Only some of these traits are to be found in Dieste's trilogy, and then greatly attenuated or overcome. The Valle-Inclan *esperpentos* (frightful or ugly dramas) and barbaric comedies contrast greatly with the Dieste trilogy marked by notable delicacy in the treatment of love and lovers. *La Nación,* however, likened *Journey* to a specific Valle-Inclán work:

> To find comparison to this excellent book of tragic and popular accent and of deep and beautiful language one must cite works of the type of *Divinas palabras* [Divine Words] by don Ramón Valle-Inclán.[13]

While it is true that some common characters may be found in the works of both playwrights—beggars, peasants, a blind man, and a pilgrim—in *Divinas palabras* (1920), the moral depravity, adultery, eroticism, and perverseness exceed anything in Dieste's trilogy. Don Frontán's wild life is only schematically suggested on stage in the playlet enacted by puppets, a poetic technique which provides aesthetic distance and debilitates any possible realistic image of perversity. There is more allusion than outright viewing. The treatment of Doña Luparia's exploitation of Rocío in the city becomes so exaggerated and outlandish that it is relatively inoffensive and in any case quickly relieved by the *deus ex machina* arrival of Sergio.

Dieste's young couples—Rocío and Sergio, Salerosa and Pinturillas—have all the freshness of young love, and those who have lost that freshness, like Rosa and Claudio, yearn to recuperate it, even if it means taking upon themselves the roles of distrustful husband and suspected wife. Ramón del Valle-Inclán's treatment of his characters is generally harsh, depreciative, and dehumanizing, making them caricatures or puppets within his well-known aesthetic attitude of subjecting reality to the deforming mathematics of the concave mirror. This results in the minimization of the audience's emotional attachment, as Robert Lima explains, "Rather than encourage empathetic response in his audiences, as did classic tragedy, Valle-Inclán opted for their objective exploration of the enigma of human existence."[14]

Dieste's attitude toward human frailty is much more compassionate, like that of his puppeteers Salerosa and Pinturillas, who become involved in their creation and in the suffering of Don Frontán. In this author there is no cynicism but rather a good deal of respect and compassion for man, prisoner of himself and his past, searching for mystery, redemption, love, or certainty in a world in which these are indeed rare gems. One may conjecture that Dieste, director of a puppet theater, must have been as carried away with the reality of his inventions as his puppeteers in *Journey*. In any case, his interest in his characters is not only intellectual, as with Valle-Inclán, but also emotional. Why else would he return to his old friends Don Frontán, Don Juan, and Doña Luparia more than a decade after creating them to rework them lovingly and give them more of himself and his experiences?

In a letter to Dieste written from Paris in 1946, Arturo Serrano Plaja speaks of what he considers the most important aspect of his work, that "pious piety" which originates in the author's own person. Some of his characters are indeed models of kindness, candor, and piety; others have a reservoir of goodness which has only to be tapped. In short, while Valle-Inclán's influence is discernible and the use of farce set in rural Galicia with strange and mysterious overtones is Valle-Inclánesque, our playwright's work responds to a view of life radically different from that of his predecessor in that he is more given to meditative and metaphysical inspiration. Dieste himself seems to have recognized the influence of his countryman in a very subtle form of homage, implied literary allusion. The puppet show presented in *Journey* bears a striking resemblance to another found in Valle-Inclán's play *Los cuernos de don Friolera* (Don Friolera's Horns, 1921), also staged at a fair and including the common theme of the cuckold who needs prodding.

Valle-Inclán's theater was not popular with the masses, but Dieste, we believe, makes an attempt to elicit the interest and response of the humble people he so often depicts in his works and who formed the audiences of his puppet shows performed under the auspices of the Pedagogical Missions. One way of accomplishing this is by building upon well-known literary tradition, using tragi-comedy and stock characters like the go-between (Dõna Luparia), the enamored old man (Don Serafín), the irresistible lover (Don Juan), and the rebellious son (Don Frontán) who are capable of surprising us and themselves, supporting the Guest's contention, "I know antiquity is born every day with the sun" (*Perdition*, 333). Characters which are at the same time old and new, an innate feeling for the dramatic, respect for the folk traditions of Galicia, expressive and lyrical prose, mystery, ambiguity, and deep concern for man's destiny (his "role") combine to make Rafael Dieste's theater both artistically and ideologically unique, not only at the time of its writing, but even today, some four decades later.

CHAPTER 5

Other Plays in Spanish

BESIDES *Journey, Duel, and Perdition*, Dieste's theater in Spanish includes two farces originally published in the volume *Breaking of Doña Luparia and Other Farces* in 1934, two others which appeared in the Loyalist magazine *Hora de España* during the Civil War, and a screen version of a story written by his brother Eduardo. As late as 1972, more than a decade after Dieste's return to Galicia, Luis Seoane noted in *La Voz de Galicia* (August 30) that the two plays written during the Civil War were still unknown in Spain. One of them *Nuevo retablo de las maravillas* (The New Spectacle of Wonders) was, however, included in the anthology *Teatro de agitación política 1933–1939* (Theater of Political Agitation) prepared by Miguel Bilbatúa and published in 1976 by Cuadernos para el Diálogo in Madrid.

I Curious Death Outwitted

In the opening scene of *Curiosa muerte burlada* the wealthy Esteban confides to his younger servant Silvestre his plan to raise his young concubine Oliva to the status of wife after testing her fidelity. He will pretend to be ruined financially and will feign death, upon which Silvestre is to court her. The servant is reluctant but Esteban insists, "Leave me alone, for I am about to begin the play" (119).[1] When Esteban informs Oliva of his losses, she is sympathetic and indignant at the suggestion that she seek a more advantagious relationship; in addition she offers her own savings. Still not satisfied, Esteban has Silvestre powder his face to make him look sick, and a peddler posing as a doctor convinces the distraught girl that Esteban is dead. Late at night before the "body" of Esteban, Silvestre confesses to Oliva his love, kept secret for years, and tells her it was his master's wish that he take care of her. Oliva resists, and as he embraces her, faints. The dead man jumps up and insults them, but Silvestre chides him, "You you are to blame for all this: that my hidden love, which is now not a fiction but the truth, became unleashed" (146). As he carries Oliva off to his mountain village, he assures Esteban, "And she will love me, she will love my firm heart that does not require so many measures for proof " (147). Esteban, desperate, calls out to Oliva but it is too late. "On the bed of the fiction he falls, overcome with sorrow" (147).

The farce is fast paced, with emphasis on plot rather than character development as in Dieste's longer plays and, as is usual in farces, verisimilitude is not a concern, although what might be called moral verisimilitude is present. In fact the plot resembles somewhat Cervantes's novelette interpolated in the *Quijote*, "El curioso impertinente" (The Impertinent Curiosity-seeker), whose title is evoked by the allusion to curiosity in that of Dieste's play. The inexplicable perversity of the husband Anselmo in the Cervantine model, who tests his wife's fidelity by asking his best friend Lothario to try to seduce her is attenuated in the farce since Oliva is not yet Esteban's wife, but the results of such a dangerous experiment are comparable to those which Cervantes describes. It should also be noted that Dieste's treatment of Oliva's rather irregular status is markedly liberal within the traditional Spanish view of morality involving a future wife.

As we shall see in *The New Spectacle of Wonders*, Dieste uses a play within the play which turns out to be true. It is a technique persistently employed in the author's theater with varied perspectives, ironic here and in *At Dawn*, therapeutic in *Journey*, prophetic in *The New Spectacle of Wonders*, and evocative in *Duel*. Silvestre plays his role in the playlet sincerely and with a pure heart, turning the fiction into life. Some people are prepared for acting by life itself, for as Esteban observes, the peddler will play his part well because of his job. Esteban finds that he has lost control over his fiction which ironically ends just as he planned.

II The Amazon and the Eccentrics

La amazona y los excéntricos, subtitled *A Little Circus Comedy*, is a light farce presenting the efforts of two clowns, Cándido and Flor, to win the favors of Casilda, the Amazon acrobatic horseback rider. The clowns vie to be considered the more valiant, the bigger liar, and the nicer, but Casilda confuses them with ambiguities by answering "you, he, you" without making it clear to whom she refers. After a series of entertaining tests, Casilda proposes that they choose between two chests which will be brought out successively, one of which will have a lion in it and the other, Casilda herself. The suitors engage in all kinds of verbal acrobatics to avoid opening the chest. Flor says the one who opens first deserves Casilda because he takes all the risks, whether the prize be Casilda or the lion. Cándido retorts that the second is no worse off, for if the other won the Amazon, he would be devoured by the lion. The Illusionist refuses to decide for them and as they flip a coin, Casilda emerges indignantly from the chest and returns; now the clowns dispute eagerly as to who will open it. They appeal to the audience which repeats Casilda's earlier ambiguities; "You, that one." Then the same chest opens again and a lion peers out, roars, laughs, and hides within again. The clowns once more ask the audience's help and the chest meantime is carried away. The other chest is carried in, the Illusionist steps out of it, and the lion tamer comes looking for his most ferocious lion whom the Illusionist calls a fake. The desperate Cándido finally decides to open the chest even if it means that Casilda has been transformed into a lion that might devour him, but he finds it empty. Nevertheless, he is willing to enter and wait for the mystery that will bring him before the girl. Flor warns him not to trust the Illusionist, for he might find a real lion. Finally he too enters the chest in pursuit of the lovers, only to find it empty. The chest is carried away to make room for Casilda's prodigious act.

This little farce is a delightful piece which can be enjoyed on an elementary level with all the clownlike antics typical of a Punch and Judy show, with the suitors hitting each other, knocking heads, dressing like dragons, and appealing to the audience. On another level, the linguistic acrobatics, quick repartee, the games of ambiguities, the rationalizations to avoid danger, and the evasive baroqueness of Casilda's answers are equally entertaining. The Amazon confuses her suitors continually, as when she says; "To the one who guesses what I'll give him, I will give what I would give if he guessed which of the two I like best" (153).[2]

Can a light circus comedy based on the eternal theme of vying for a woman's favor be anything more than a farce? In this respect it should be remembered that the circus clown's humor is, in the finest representations, accompanied by a certain degree of pathos in the Charlie Chaplin tradition. It is obvious in the play that each one can see only his own view which assures him that he is more worthy and loves Casilda more, but who can decide such questions? Then, too, we find ourselves laughing at some all-too-typical characteristics of human behavior such as talking rather than acting, letting the other fellow go first where there is danger, wanting to put difficult decisions into the hands of others (or of destiny), and entering into clownlike behavior for love. The insistence of each clown to outdo the other might have gone on indefinitely were it not for the decision of Cándido (in accordance with his name which means "candid") to put his trust in the Illusionist's tricks, to believe even when he finds nothing. Perhaps in all these antics there is a subtle parable of life which continually confronts us with the problematic task of choosing, with its illusions, dangers, and hopes, and with the final vision of emptiness, like an empty chest in whose darkness we desperately hope to find a miracle.

III   At Dawn

The one-act play *Al amanecer*, set in a town large enough to have a bishop and a castle, opens with a conversation between the Marquis of Piedraquemada (Burntstone) and his sister who indignantly recall voices of popular protest. The Marquis feels the fatigue of a decrepit nobility before those voices which make him feel almost ashamed of his family crests. His sister Jacinta defends "Spanish integrity" being served by the scientific extermination practiced by Teuton and Italian "specialists" asisting in the defense of their cause. They are joined by the young philosopher Pascalín (little Pascal, recalling the seventeenth-century French philosopher), Adela Medina—concerned about contradictory news of her husband's column—and then Bishop Capellini, the millionaire Cayetano Echave, and finally Captain Agüero, ostensibly an enemy but secretly a Nationalist like themselves. Echave announces the arrival of "a village woman with signs of being pregnant" (105), who is none other than Adela's husband, Lieutenant Medina, disguised to carry out a mission.[3] As the women and Pascalín go for wine, the soldiers brief the other men on the ambush of "Red" or Loyalist troops planned to take place when Captain Agüero will lead them to the plaza in front of the Marquis' palace. In preparation for the ambush, Agüero enacts the scene of how he will beg his colonel to let him die for the "Republic of workers." Despite the merriment of the others, the Marquis remains perplexed and tormented. Agüero explains that one contingent will be situated in the palace and others in the intersections. The Marquis is relieved to let the Bishop direct him and, assured of their success, the latter promotes Agüero half in jest to the rank of general. Agüero in turn addresses Medina as "Commander" and the women become the "honorary Red Cross."

At dawn the voice of Agüero is heard leading the militiamen to rest in the plaza. He enters the palace to await the ambush sign but it never comes, so he himself fires the shot. Machine guns and cries are heard offstage; obstinate voices shout "traitors!" Realizing that things have gone sour, the Bishop and the millionaire deny their part in the situation, but the treacherous Agüero will not let them. The Marquis is hit by a bullet from the plaza as Agüero cries, "Every man for himself!" He is heard offstage again telling the militiamen that he has found the traitors, but he is shot. In panic Echave suggests to the Bishop that they play dead. Republican militiamen kick the "corpses," seem convinced, and leave. The rest is in pantomime as the Bishop and Echave, after a prudent wait, begin to raise themselves, infinitely shocked to see rifle barrels pointing at them as two militiamen advance silently "with the inevitability of dawn" before their frenzied cries of terror.

The play was performed in the Teatro Español in Madrid with María Bru playing Jacinta and Espantaleón as Echave. Dieste recalls that the great musician Enrique Casal Chapí chose both the choral chant—not a revolutionary piece but simply a peasant song—which the militiamen sing and the contrasting turn-of-the-century polka which Jacinta plays on the old palace piano, enhancing the noticeable difference between the two groups portrayed. Unlike other Dieste plays, At Dawn takes place at a very precise historical moment, in July 1936, generally considered the outbreak of the Spanish Civil War with the rebellion of military forces in Africa which spread to the Peninsula. The piece itself was published almost two years later in Hora de España (March, 1938), which prefaced its monthly edition with ominous references to the difficulties faced by the loyal Republicans and encouraging hopes of victory:

Our Spain is passing through one of the most bitter critical moments of the war.

The German and Italian invaders, on the pretext of helping Franco, want to seize power in all of Spain and are attacking furiously on the Aragon front, supported by fantastic quantities of war matériel. Our soldiers struggle heroically to contain the enemy advance. All loyal Spain vibrates excitedly in these moments . . .

Our triumph will be the result of present pain. And our victory, which we must offer the world, will someday be a source of pride for those who fought and shame for those who would not help us effectively in such dire times.

At *Dawn* was obviously intended to respond to the urgent moment of crisis and to serve as inspiration for the Republican cause and for an ultimate victory. In the art of propaganda there are two ways of depicting the problem. The author may choose to focus upon his own side, in which case he is apt to show its virtues and heroism in a serious vein. On the other hand, portrayal of the opposition provides an opportunity for satire and ridicule so that one's own forces are by implication seen as superior. This is the posture that Dieste adopts in his farce by characterizing a representative group of Nationalists (nobility, eccelesiastic authority, the wealthy, and the military) preparing the ambush of Loyalist forces whose voices are heard collectively offstage. It is significant that they are not portrayed as individuals, but rather as a cohesive group, in contrast to the Nationalists in the palace who are quick to disclaim responsibility when things go wrong and to resort to anything to save their individual scalps.

The enemy is portrayed in a farcical fashion, appearing ridiculous and absurd, though Dieste shows some compassion for poor old Marquis Burntstone who at least recognizes his weakness as the last dry bough on a family tree of yester-year's aristocracy. He hears with trepidation but without anger the popular voices of protest which threaten his position, while his sister defends the nobility's right to perpetuate its status with the intervention of the "exterminating angels"—the Germans, Italians, and Moors. The other characters, in need of the Marquis' palace and dwindling funds, pay little or no heed to him. When he does do something, such as alerting the doormen, the Bishop comments with tremendous irony, "you're pure fire, Marquis, pure fire" (113), as the latter smiles like a corpse. He is the first to be hit by a bullet, but in his case it seems more like a *coup de grace*.

Pascalín, whom Jacinto introduces as the "newest philosopher of old Spain," (102), offers theories about the role of his Nationalists, "it is the Western Christian culture that finally, abandoning the marasmus of tolerance in which it was about to succumb, opposes its invincible energy against the Asiatic hordes" (102). Despite his propensity for hyperbole which sees Medina as a courageous Ulysses, he is occasionally capable of perceiving the irony, if not the absurdity, of the situation as he ponders the enthusiasm with which the Nationalists welcome the arrival of Moorish troops, "How mysterious is history. Who would have said to the Crusaders that Moors were going to save Christian civilization!" (111), recalling the seven-century struggle of Christian Spain to expel the Moors. He is of little importance, however, as the diminutive form of his name would suggest, and is sent away with the women when military strategy is being planned. He eagerly places himself in the hands of the Bishop, feeling amply protected by the enormous scapulary the latter gives him.

The Bishop, who considers the conflict a holy war, offers reassurance with prayers and scapularies. From his position high above the marauding masses he feels safe and sure that the "tumultuous sea will stay down there" (115). The Marquis is more realistic, "But splashes may get up here." Agüero, the traitor, is defined by the Bishop as "one of the few paladins of Christ who still has the devil's confidence" (107). The characters in the parody, however, are not grossly exaggerated or reduced to symbolism; their weaknesses are very human ones.

The play has values that transcend its intent as propaganda, for the author's innate sense of art and his intellectual interests would not be content with mere subordination to practical circumstance. For example, the whole idea of role playing in the tradition of Calderón de la Barca's famous title, *The Great Theater of Life*, acquires special meaning. *At Dawn* portrays what might be called "The Great Theater of War" involving such forms of pretense as disguises, masks, playacting, betrayal, and delusions of grandeur. It is interesting to note that in popular use the expression "*teatro de la guerra*" or "theater of war" means front or scene of military action. The expression captures perfectly Dieste's vision in *At Dawn* of war as theater involving playacting of various sorts in which an unconvincing performance can be fatal indeed.

Early in the play the Marquis sees his sister and himself as having no roles, "We are two masks or two empty names" (100). Later on he comments, "Titles are of little importance when they can no longer be enhoyed" (111). There is farce in the appearance of Lieutenant Medina, disguised as a pregnant peasant woman, swearing on the sword he isn't carrying—for obvious reasons—that Captain Agüero is an honorable hero. There is theater of fantasy as Bishop Capellini bestows the titles of General and Commander upon Agüero and Medina while the others join in these premature delusions.

Dieste again uses his characteristic theater within theater technique with great effectiveness. We have noted that *At Dawn* depicts the opposing camp, but within this framework there is a playlet in which the Nationalists parody Dieste's own group, the Loyalists, when Captain Agüero acts out the part of a faithful Republican commander asking his superior (played by Medina, now in military dress) to be allowed to risk his life. The scene is tremendously ironic when one remembers that Dieste intended Republican actors to play the part of the Nationalist characters Agüero and Medina, who in this scene portray Republicans. The confusion which often results from the demands of war may best be expressed in Adela Medina's words upon finding her friends after being lost in the palace corridors, "I was in an attic; I tripped across some mirrors . . . I don't know! This palace is a labyrinth" (103). The Marquis adds, "good for playing hide and seek," summarizing most appropriately the hide-and-seek nature of war, where mirrors are relegated to attics because they reflect the truth, which in times of crisis is often cast side.

For Pascalín, the ambush plot being carried out by the suddenly promoted "General" Agüero and "Commander" Medina makes sense only as a play, "I am beginning to understand. It is . . . a play" (114). Medina corrects him calling it an important war operation and Pascalín, inspired by the scapulary—which may be considered a theater prop—commits himself to the Bishop, who serves as director of the scene. The Marquis, with no role to play, is as confused as Pascalín as to who is betraying whom and what is being betrayed, and comes to a similar conclusion regarding Agüero, "Maybe he is acting out a farce" (118). The militiamen who kill Agüero were obviously not convinced by his acting and confront the traitor with the words, "Hands up, *farsante*," which means both "fake" and "actor in a farce," underscoring the ambiguity between war and theater which has been cultivated in the play.

A final theatrical performance within *At Dawn* occurs as the panicked Bishop and Echave play dead. The militiamen who kick the "corpses" and rejoice at having saved themselves trouble and ammunition are a convinced audience. The two actors congratulate themselves for their successful performance, but find that not everyone has gone home after the show, as two militiamen punish their duplicity with death. All the actors in the several farces within the play are Nationalists, while the Republicans play no roles but their own and (belying history) ultimately triumph.

IV   The New Spectacle of Wonders

In the opening scene of the play *Nuevo retablo de las maravillas* we see paraphernalia for repairing a road as three workers discuss their fears of quitting early although they are exhausted, not wanting to give the authorities about to arrive a pretext to mistreat them. "If you, hammers that oppress us, were only guns!" one exclaims (170).[4] They leave and three other characters arrive— Fantasio, who is a minstrel, charlatan, acrobat, and prestidigitator; his wife Mónica, dancer and accordionist; and their apprentice Rabelín. Meeting with the distrust of the villagers, Fantasio explains, "We have to lie in order to live, that's all" (173). A country girl warns that they have come to a bad place, for "they" are in control there and "even in nightmares one does not see such horrors" (175). Fearful of the approaching dignitaries, the villagers leave. The Mayor, a Landowner, the Priest, a young Gentleman with two women, the General, and the Marchioness find Fantasio very immersed in some work with a strange apparatus and inquire about his activities. Fantasio lists his academic degrees, feigning modesty and explaining that he is setting up his latest invention which has provided invaluable services to the police—a spectacle that can only be seen by "those who are untainted by Marxism, syndicalism, anarchy, and other plagues" (181). The Priest suspects the devil's work but all agree to view the show.

Fantasio announces each spectacle as the audience pretends to see all he describes and more. "Let us be faithful to the old model respected by Cervantes" (186), says the stage manager Fantasio, announcing the appearance of a bull—which the General fights— rats, and lizards to the consternation of the women. At the request of the Priest for something more traditional, Fantasio's spectacle now purports to show the arrival of three thousand Protestant, German, and Moorish troops, whom the General salutes as saviors of Spain before the general enthusiasm of the others. The minstrel passes his hat for contributions, but all excuse themselves except the General who offers a German postwar bill which Fantasio in turn offers to an invisible Moor. The mayor, as in Cervantes's model, asks if it is necessary to prepare quarters to house the troops. Rabelín plays the Communist "Internationale" hymn on his accordion. The Priest tries to break the spell he thinks Rabelín is under, and the latter breaks out in the Royal March, which pleases the audience. Mónica, however, announces an invasion by Red militiamen and the frightened dignitaries hide under the women's skirts, as the General requests reinforcements with an invisible telephone.

The militiamen are scared off (by the Marchioness's presence, according to Rabelín) and Fantasio announces the advance on Madrid, which the General leads on a cardboard horse. Their jubilant victory is cut short by the villagers who come armed with hammers, sickles, and pitchforks, followed by thousands of militiamen. "It is the truth of the spectacle unleashed," (202) comments Mónica. The authorities are driven away and Fantasio says, "The land is purified. Art begins anew. I renounce my inventions. I can only dance" (203). The bugle player Cornetín pleads to be permitted to join them. For Fantasio "true marvels are seen when eyes are clear and free" and the play ends with the waving of a red handkerchief, the playing of the "Internationale," and raised fists.

We are obviously dealing with a propaganda farce, and yet there is none of the naturalistic representation we might expect in political theater. Dieste prefers distancing techniques which allow more intellectual contemplation than emotional involvement. He joins comic satire of the type Aristophanes used for critical purposes with the puppet show (although the puppets of the spectacle are invisible), and the theme of the common people versus the injustices of the nobles which is traditional in Spanish classical theater. The use of farce in itself frees the author from the restraints of verisimilitude which realistic drama imposes. We perceive in the exaggerated antics of the characters an essential ambience of unreality which permits a certain detachment as we watch them, without identifying ourselves with them as human beings. Thus we can see things more clearly and receive the message more directly.

The elements of farce are equally distributed between actions and dialogues. Fantasio's statement of qualifications, for example, ridicules the young Gentleman who says he is a lawyer, "Experience of the world, physiognomic science, telepathy, animal magnetism and other arts in which I was instructed in Munich, confirmed in Bologna, graduated in Coimbra, blessed in Rome and aspergilated in Burgos" (179). Scenes such as the General on a cardboard horse, and hiding under the Marchioness's skirt, as well as exaggerated blows and grotesque positions add to the farcical tone.

Dieste's chief distancing technique, however, is allusion to Cervantes's original one-act play, *Entremés del retablo de las maravillas* (Farce of the Spectacle of *Wonders*) which allows us to observe a new rendering of a well-known work and invites us to equate the Fascist view of Spain with that of inquisitorial Spain in Cervantes's time. In the original *Spectacle of Wonders*, Chanfalla and Chirinos are the tricksters; the dupes are the Governor, Mayor, Municipal Secretary, Councilman, and two women. Chanfalla, the stage manager, explains that only legitimate offspring and pure-blooded Christians (as opposed to converts) can see the spectacle composed by Tontonelo (equivalent to Dumbbell) the Wise. The spectacle purports to show Samson about to tear down the columns of the temple, a bull, rats from Noah's ark, rain from the fount of the River Jordan, lions, bears, and the dancer Herodias. The audience pretends to see because of "honor," and a quartermaster interrupts the show to order the Governor to prepare quarters for thirty soldiers. The audience thinks this, too, is one of Chanfalla's creations. When the quartermaster denies seeing anything in the spectacle since he has not been informed of its significance, he becomes the object of ridicule. He brandishes his sword and riotous fighting breaks out. Chanfalla is so convinced of the effectiveness of his spectacle that he resolves to show it the next day to the whole town.

The question of Jewish ancestry was an important issue in Cervantes's Spain and legitimacy was essential in order to trace one's background to prove himself "untainted" by Semitic ancestry. Dieste's concern is with an equally relevant question of the late 1930's—the Fascist aversion to various factions which supported the Republican cause. He does perhaps go overboard on the symbolism at the end, but in view of the red-hot political situation this can be understood and condoned in a farce. It is after all theater of propaganda and agitation, and to Dieste's credit he was able to distinguish the situation as a basic human one, not unique to one particular moment of Spain's history or literature. We realize, in fact, that the theme of people's deluding themselves to conform to behavioral patterns dictated by others did not originate with Cervantes either, being a traditional folk motif found also in Juan Manuel's fourteenth-century story "El paño maravilloso" (The Wonderful Cloth). It exists, too, in other literature, such as Hans Christian Andersen's tale "The Emperor's New Clothes."

Dieste adheres to some of Cervantes's techniques in addition to that of a play within a play, including using names which are humorous puns or merely generic designations. Cervantes's dupes are the Governor and his aldermen Repollo (Cabbage), Castrado

(Eunuch), and Capacho (Hamper-top), while Chanfalla works with Chirinos (Trifles or Happy-go-lucky). The apprentice who provides music is the same in both works, Rabelín, meaning small player of the rebeck, a three-stringed instrument played with a bow. Dieste's characters embrace a wider scope of ecclesiastical, social, and political representatives—the Priest who takes off his miter so his parishoners won't notice him in their tumultuous attack, the ambitious Gentleman who sees himself as Minister of War, the pompous Marchioness, opportunist women such as Tarasca (Brazen) and Remilgada (Prim), the General, Landlord, and Cornetín (Bugle Player). Fantasio's name indicates his gift for creating fantastic illusions.

There are some essential differences between the Cervantine model and Dieste's reworking of the farce. In the original, the audience confuses reality with illusion, thinking that the quartermaster and soldiers are part of the spectacle, while in the *New Spectacle* the people are carried away by the fantasy itself, confusing illusion with reality when they think the Red troops have run away, and they prepare to enter Madrid triumphantly. Then the Cervantine arrival of real soldiers is repeated when the militiamen appear and, as Mónica says, the truth of the spectacle is unleashed. The audience's reaction in Dieste's play is similar to that of Cervantes's work, and in both there is the sharp satire of the double folly which the foolish authorities incur by falling victim to the illusion imposed by others (the stage manager and society) and to self-deception.

Perhaps the greatest advantage of the theater within the theater technique is that it leaves us, the real audience or readers, in yet another dimension beyond both that of the victims and the creator of the illusion. On our level the question of reality is more complex, for we can see that the illusions Fantasio projects are indeed real in Spain during the Civil War. The combined army of Moors and Germans which the audience in the play pretends to see is not real in the show but exists in the real world outside the farce so that the larger audience and we as readers, observing what Calderón called "the great theater of life," are well aware of the truth of Fantasio's illusion. The theme of reality is further complicated when Fantasio hands the German money to an invisible Moor, for it proves that even "reality" which proceeds from sense perception can be illusive. The postwar bill can be seen and touched, but ironically it is no more real than the invisible Moor since it has no function or value as money. There is also some doubt as to what a real Marxist is, since Fantasio says that "there are more Marxists than one thinks; some, perhaps the most dangerous, are Marxists without even knowing it" (181).

Dieste's farce turns out to be a well-aimed political ploy, for we, the outside audience, cannot see the tableau either, nor do we feel obligated to resort to self-deception, which places us implicitly among the "good guys" who suffer from Marxist blindness. The Cervantes scheme invites even further inferences in the context of the Civil War: If all these representatives of the social, political, and ecclesiastical orders are so easily deceived by a minstrel puppeteer, it is because they are already fools duped into being Fascists by their own ambition and that of their allies.

V *"Promise of the Old Man and the Maiden"*

Dieste wrote a screen version of a story by the same title, "Promesa del viejo y de la doncella," written by his brother Eduardo and published in 1935. It involves a lawyer, doctor, and hotel keeper who arrange the marriage of the ailing old landowner Don Juan Varona to the lawyer's innocent young niece Carmen so that the old man's hefty estate will not go to his bachelor brother or family in the city. Struggling to keep Don Juan on his feet long enough to go through with the wedding, they anticipate their own gain from the marriage. The maiden, however, turns out to be noble and sensitive, and promises the dying Don Juan that he will live in her eyes and will see wonders. He lasts long enough to announce before the gauchos that his estate will go to his wife. When Carmen's former playboy sweetheart returns to the widow, he suggests that they be lovers and enjoy the good life abroad. With a flash of her whip, she sends him off and, mounted on Varona's best horse, takes charge of everything, promising the gauchos a common share in the land if they become good workers, husbands, and family men.

As the title would suggest, the story is a Uruguayan version of the age-old theme in Spanish literature (Cervantes, Moratín) of an old man's arranged marriage to a young wife. Careful attention is given to camera directions, in capturing faraway landscape and close-up of details, with special emphasis on musical effects and subtle imagery—birds in flight, a cuckoo clock, a skull, a child's face, and a bull. Descriptions of characters are extravagant at times, "the fawning Eulalia and the leporine Escancia" (258) recalling the rich, verbal stage directions of Valle-Inclán.[5] An interesting inversion in which the camera first focuses on the interior of a house seen from outside and then a view of the countryside seen from inside the same house anticipates a similar change in perspectives which occurs in Dieste's later story "Juana Rial, Flowering Lemon Tree" in *Félix Muriel*. Typical of the author's theater is the presence of mirrors—The immobile Juan Varona is seen before a mirror, but it is more as if the mirror is looking at him. Here too we find playacting in the pretense of the plotters who are three false masks with "empty, pallid, funereal grimaces"(270).

CHAPTER 6

Loving Red Lantern

SOON after settling in Buenos Aires, Dieste published *Rojo farol amante* (Loving Red Lantern, 1940), an enlarged edition of a volume of poems published under the same title seven years earlier in Madrid. The book was greeted by the critics with enthusiasm not only in Spanish cultural circles established in the Argentine capital but also in publications as prestigious as *La Nación, El Sol,* and *El Mundo.* It remains Dieste's only published book of verse and was undoubtedly written in Spain, for as one review observed, "It has all the vigor of having been written in Castille by a spirit as genuinely Galician as that of Rafael Dieste." [1] There are no allusions to historical circumstance in these poems, for they represent an interior portrait of the author in his relationship to self, the mysteries of life and nature, and other people. Since the author has not continued in this lyrical vein, *Loving Red Lantern* is of particular interest as it expresses in this artistic medium many of the same themes, attitudes, and concerns of his other writings, especially the dramatic works with preceded its publication and *Historias e invenciones de Félix Muriel* (Stories and Inventions of Felix Muriel) which followed only three years later. The intimate connection between Dieste's poems and the stories of *Félix Muriel* was in fact noted by Esther de Cáceres in a paper read before *Reuniones de Estudio* (Study Meetings) in Montevideo on May 15, 1944, when she referred to the "music of a youthful past," and cited several poems from *Loving Red Lantern.*

I Wonders and Miracles

The tender and sensitive wonder toward the little miracles of life and nature which is a recurrent attitude in the poems of *Loving Red Lantern* prefigures what we shall call "the memorable world of Félix Muriel." Although the poem which provides the title *Loving Red Lantern* appears toward the end of the book, it is very similar to the cherry-colored lamp which serves as introduction to the memories and inventions of Félix Muriel in that it goes far beyond being a specific and concrete source of light, imparting infinite promise, affirmation, and harmony for the poet, and at the same time evoking a past which can became present: "Instante, volverás, / contigo volveré" (Instant, you will return, / with you I shall return [47]).[2] The poet compares it to a "silent miner / in the rock of air," with light both within and without "like the angel." The little lantern seems almost as wonderful as the sun: "Farolillo en la punta/del sí maravilloso / más allá del desastre" (Little lantern on the tip / of the marvelous "yes" / immune from disaster). Its importance there next to the sea is very personal for the poet: "El día está en la noche. / Noche sólo nocturna / con mi luz no se ve" (Day is in night. / Night that is only nocturnal / with my light cannot be seen).

The author has clarified the specific inspiration of this poem as follows:

Like the title of the poem, the expression alludes to an authentic lantern located at the tip of a long, jagged breakwater which attracted me with a very significant enchantment, making me walk toward it at first with restraint and then running, in danger of breaking a leg or perhaps my head on the edges of the blocks.[3]

The sensations expressed by the poet are derived directly from this real and immediate experience which, transformed into verse, transcends both time and space.

Dieste is capable of perceiving light not only in this marvelous lamp of memories and promises but also in other simple things such as early cherries, "the model of first love," in "Canción" (Song, 5):

Su luz de adentro era firme
y leve, denso primor
de la fruta recordando
que ha sido y ha de ser flor.

Su luz de adentro era firme,
su luz de afuera, licor,
zumo de esperanza,
promesa en color.

Its light within was firm
and slight, dense delight
of the fruit remembering
that it has been and will be flower.

Its light within was firm,
its light without, liqueur,
juice of hope,
promise in color.

Very much akin to the wonders of the red lantern and these cherries filled with music are the marvels which the poet discovers in "Semilla" (Seed, 36), all immanence and promise of "all possible music," new words, love, pain, and mysterious signs being forged within the seed's hidden flame.

Nature provides inspiration for the poet's childlike surprise and admiration in small wonders like rain, echoes, mountains, shores, the sun, and the sea. In "Esfera de sol marino" (Sphere of Marine Sun, 3), he exclaims:

¿No habéis visto? ¡el barco
sobre el agua!
y el sol bajo la quilla sosegado!
y los ojos del niño, desnudos,
en el sol verdemar buceando!

> Haven't you seen? The ship
> on the water!
> and the sun under the keel in calm!
> and the child's eyes naked,
> in the sea-green sun diving!

The exclamatory tone before a scene which only the eyes of the beholder find extraordinary reflects childlike wonder like that of Félix Muriel and the old man who speaks with the devil in one of his "stories and inventions." The scene is immobile but the child's eyes are in motion, diving, penetrating with candid nudity into an indistinguishable marvel of sun and sea, blended surrealistically into one.

"Perenne instante" (Perennial Instant, 14), a title which may well be applied to Dieste's plays *Journey* and *Duel* and to stories of Félix Muriel, also evokes a "recuerdo niño" (childhood memory) in Galicia, playing in the meadow with the sea below which . . .

de sí mismo no sabe
mi asombro iluminado:
la misma luz, el mismo
júbilo por lo alto
del cielo y en los ojos
niños, de sí olvidados:

of itself does not know
my illuminated wonder:
the same light, the same
delight for the height
of the sky and in the eyes so
childish, unaware of themselves.

Like the cherry-colored lamp in Félix Muriel's house, the beloved red lantern, the early cherries, and the "sphere of marine sun" previously mentioned, the "perennial instant" is seen as spherical, like a magic crystal ball filled with visions of light, memory, and hope.

One cannot help recalling the Guest's comment in *Perdition of Dona Luparia* that "antiquity is born every day with the sun" and feeling the sensation of "perennial miracle" that Juan Gil-Albert finds in that play, on reading several of Dieste's poems.[4] In "Sol serafín" (Seraphic Sun, 35), nature's daily miracles, those of remotest antiquity, are graced with religious terminology, Child Sun, Saint Morning, Saint Noon, and the titular Seraphic Sun which on dying bleeds promises and roses for the next day. Although there is some disheartenment on the part of the poet as to his own uncertain future, beholding such miracles in "El alma era confiada" (The Soul Was Confident, 34), means that each day born with the sun is seen as a miracle by the awakening soul:

El alma era confiada.	The soul was confident.
Sumida en sueños tendía	Submerged in dreams it
soñadoras las manos	stretched its dreaming
hacia la madrugada.	hands toward dawn.

| Y era siempre un milagro puntual | And the new day was always |
| el nuevo día. | a punctual miracle. |

The poem "Hombre" (Man, 9) celebrates in a manner reminiscent of Walt Whitman the awareness of the different parts of the body, eyes, head, legs, shoulders, and arms which enable man to experience and discover the wonders of the world around him, of earth, air, nearness and distance, plants and the sea: "La boca, y la nariz, / y la piel, demostraban / la existencia del aire" (The mouth, and the nose, / and the skin demonstrated / the existence of the air). But what is strange is the fact that the verbs are all in the past, producing a sensation of nostalgia for things lost, yet not devoid of hope: "Era vuelo amoroso el salto, / libertad el destino, / y la memoria—aquella y esta, / resucitada—, vaticinio" (The jump was loving flight, / destiny freedom, / and memory—that one and this, / reborn—, prophecy).

In "Bajo el cielo del padre" (Under the Father's Sky, 13) a drama of nature filled with small miracles reflects the incomprehensible drama of the poet's spirit (or of man's in general) in the opposition of a lovely flower and a dark pool:

La flor maravillosa	The marvelous flower
y el enturbiado estanque	and the darkened pool
se miraban pasmados	looked at each other in wonder
bajo el cielo del padre.	under the father's sky,

y en el cielo una dura	and in the sky a hard
sonrisa inexplicable	unexplainable smile
detenía los barcos	was stopping the ships,
endureciendo el aire,	hardening the air,

mas vuela un pajarillo	but a little bird flies
que de aquello no sabe	knowing nothing of all that
y, repentino, suelta	and suddenly frees
la brisa entre los árboles.	the breeze among the trees.

The opposition is both exterior, observed in nature, and interior, representing to the poet corresponding forces in man's spirit. The little bird, on the other hand, is unaware of such spiritual tension and in his happy innocence creates his own little miracle.

It is not only in nature that Dieste finds reasons for amazement, but also in the contemplation of life itself and its natural consequence, death:

No me verás triste	You will not see me sad
sino maravillado.	but rather in wonder.
En barco de nacer	On the ship of birth
y morir, embarcado.	and death embarked.

| Quien muere y resucita | He who dies and is reborn |
| se embarca en el milagro. | embarks upon a miracle. (30) |

He feels that one may be reborn toward death and expresses this in terms of a voyage with a route of double destination, continuing the sustained marine imagery and quiet tone so reminiscent of Alfred Lord Tennyson's famous poem "Crossing the Bar". For Dieste, the marvelous is the result of not knowing; only the unknown and the unfathomable are worthy of being called miracles, and he concludes:

Mas yo no sé hacia dónde resucito
ni el nombre
de mis astros
ni hacia dónde me lleva
la nave del milagro.
¡Si vinieras
          conmigo!

> But I know not the direction of my rebirth
> or the name
> of my stars
> or the direction in which the ship
> of miracles takes me.
> If you could only come
>   with me!

Although the poet at the close of these verses would wish to be accompanied, generally his verses of wonder seem steeped in solitude, with only two protagonists, himself and the world about him. The relationship of self, a major theme in the book, to this outside world is treated in one of the most extensive poems in *Loving Red Lantern*: "Reconocimiento" (Recognition, 31), in which he views with quiet amazement his own body outside of him as if it were a little tree offering the "cup of its innocence to the sun":

> Me sorprendió que el arbolito
> no tuviese raíces
> o las tenga tan elásticas
> que puede andar sobre la tierra
> en cascarones mecánicos
> ir al polo norte
> girar subir y bajar
> en la tierra en el aire y en el agua

>   It surprised me that the little tree
>   had no roots
>   or had them so elastic
>   that it could walk on the land
>   in mechanical shells
>   go to the North Pole
>   turn go up and go down
>   on land in the air and in water.

He observes steel bones which seem to be as much a product of a mechanical nature as of human ingenuity and inventiveness, since they can be seen outside of man "like his body and his machines." But he also has seen that the hurricane could carry away the little tree and fire consume it. He expresses the harmony of the interior and exterior being in an affectionate contemplation of the self in direct contact with nature, objects, and creativity, realizing that "I am not its prison." This is the marvel of the self, which is within and

without, controlled yet free to cover the outside world and return to
the harmony of body and mind in one "filial heart."

A final miracle which Dieste celebrates in this book of poems is
that of creation itself in "Sorpresa del molinero" (The Miller's
Surprise, 4):

Hiciste un molino creyendo que sólo para moler trigo.	You made a mill thinking that it was only to grind wheat.
El agua encauzaste creyendo que sólo para que trabaje.	You channelled the water thinking that it was only for it to work.
Pero el agua dice sentencias y coplas que no le pediste.	But the water says sentences and songs that you did not ask for.
Y al agua responde pensativo y lírico el molino dócil.	And to the water responds pensive and lyrical the docile mill.
Haciendo un molino y encauzando el agua dibujaste un signo.	By making a mill and channelling the water you drew a sign.
Y absorto investigas viendo la molienda lo que significa.	And you investigate entranced seeing the milling what it means.

The poem is valuable as an expression of *ars poetica*, revealing
Dieste's attitude toward his creation. Like the water of the mill, the
materials of literary creation may surprise the writer and thus lead
him to expressing things he is not even aware of. This is the
experience Mr. Baldomero recounts in *The Empty Window*, finding
a piece of redwood on an island and whittling it with the intention of
carving a saint only to find to his amazement that the wood had
dictated its own form, that of a devil. The creator may go about his
work with specific intent and channel his materials in accordance
with these intentions but the final product may elude even his
comprehension, acquiring a mystery all its own which may surprise
the artist as well as the observer or reader. The act of creating, then,
is not conclusive but rather a source of wonder, mystery, and
revelation to be investigated even by the artist himself.

In a great number of Dieste's poems there is frequent use of
diminutive forms suggestive of simple, childlike wonder before
"little miracles" in the poet's world: *pajarillo, nubecillas, viente-
cillo, arbolito, campanita, florecilla, farolillo,* etc. (little bird,
clouds, wind, tree, bell, flower, lantern. The diminutive in Spanish
conveys a feeling of affection as well as indicating small size).

II *The Theme of Self-encounter*

The greatest single theme, expressed in several subthemes, is
that of self-encounter forming an important link between the poems
of *Loving Red Lantern* and the rest of Dieste's creative work.
Sometimes the encounter is strange and unexpected, as in
"Esquina" (Corner, 10), in which the poet describes his meeting
with "the hostile face without eyes" that smiles at him without lips.
The face waiting on the corner declares that it is his shadow and
complains of being forgotten. His message is given in words that
dissolve and the poet concludes:

La cara de mi sombra,	The face of my shadow,
encontrada o perdida,	found or lost,
no es así: sólo eres	is not so: you are at most
la cara de la esquina.	the face of the corner.

It is difficult to distinguish precisely where one's own self begins
and the outside world ends, whether one's shadow really belongs to
him or to the surface upon which it is cast.

Similar to "Corner" is "Vieja ciudad" (Old City, 18), in which the
word shadow reappears several times: "Or maybe I am my shadow,"
"the shadow of this old city does not greet me," "on naked shadow I
must die, being born." Life seems to be an old city whose horizons
are a blind wall (death) and in which:

. . . he de ser aventura
y riesgo de no ser quien soy,
fuera de mí cambiando de figura

> . . . I must be adventure
> and the risk of not being who I am,
> outside myself changing my figure

The poet sees himself "suddenly unexpected and without sense /

for the plan / of a supposed destiny." To find one's destiny in a city
as old as humanity and as mysterious as life and death is no easy
matter:

> Es duro, sí, tal vez mortal, buscar de nuevo
> melódica razón
> o capricho frenético
> desde cada ciudad al universo.

> It is hard, and even perhaps fatal, to seek again
> melodical reason
> or frenetic caprice
> from each city to the universe.

In both "Corner" and "Old City" there is a desire to seek
confirmation of personal existence in the outside world in which one
projects himself and his uncertain destiny. As we have seen in
"Reconocimiento" (Recognition, 31), the poet is able to distinguish
his own form as a part of that world which his senses perceive, and
marvels at his ability to venture into the world without and return to
harmony with the self within.

In the following poem, number 32, the poet looks toward the sky
which becomes a series of possibilities that might confirm his
existential aloneness or promise some hope:

¿Eres tú o sólo espejo?　　　　　Is it you or only a mirror?

¿Eres en soledad espectro　　　　Are you in solitude a spectre
de mi esperanza única　　　　　　of my only hope
de cabal universo?　　　　　　　for a perfect universe?

¿Eres de mi nostalgia　　　　　　Are you of my nostalgia
solitario el eco,　　　　　　　　the solitary echo,
cenobita en ladera de monte　　　cenobite on a mountain side
de silencio?　　　　　　　　　　of silence?

¿Eres quizá un deseo,　　　　　　Are you perhaps a wish,
entre pálidas nubes barquero?　　 boatman among pale clouds?

¿Eres　　　　　　　　　　　　Are you
el que fuí　　　　　　　　　　　the one I was
el que seré　　　　　　　　　　the one I will be
mirándome?　　　　　　　　　watching myself?

¿O de azares de luz,	Or of accidents of light,
en mi instante,	in my moment,
alegórico juego?	an allegorical game?
¡Mírame	Look at me
cielo!	sky!

The second stanza in particular suggests the story of Félix Muriel entitled "La peña y el pájaro" (The Rock and the Bird) in which the protagonist Anselmo encounters the cenobite Andrés in his search for himself and for knowledge, and at the end a voice with echoes of the mountain answers Anselmo's anguished cry. The story is a narrative treatment of the same questions the poet asks about his origin, his destiny, and reality.

Dieste's concern with his relationship to the things around him is a perpetual source of wonder. The solitary rider of poem number twenty-three finds himself in an "immobile theater of rocks" and feels his bones in "mineral fraternity" with the rocks which serve as mirrors. In "Espacio entre paredes" (Space Between Walls, 42) he again considers the question of where he begins and the outside world ends, but it is in this exploration and experience with the world that one comes to know himself better. This is expressed in "Perenne pasajero" (Perennial Passenger, 2) as a simple paradox; "Buscaba el corazón / hacia fuera de sí / cada vez más adentro" (He looked for his heart / outside himself / ever more within.)

Self-encounter in *Loving Red Lantern* is not limited to considerations of the poet's past and present, but also includes the contemplation of death, "the mute and fast / river of dead water" ("Ultimo recelo" [Last Fear, 15]). In the closing poem of the volume, the poet proposes the possibility that some vague "something" may silence his voice but that "someone for me would say, / speaking like the wind / that speaks for the tree":

Aquí están	Here are
estas tablas,	these planks,
esta orilla, esta cáscara	this shore, this shell
salada, esta osamenta—	of salt, these bones—

But the post mortem is not devoid of hope, for the poem ends with the victorious liberating flight of a bird, a recurrent image also found in "Primer viaje por mejillas," (First Trip through Cheeks, 6) and in "Bajo el cielo del padre" (Under the Father's Sky, 13):

y acaso un repentino	and perhaps a sudden
pájaro no vencido,	bird undefeated
con su breve ganancia	with his brief gain
con su menuda eternidad de oro	with his small eternity of gold
con mil mañanas claras	with a thousand clear tomorrows
y riberas cantoras	and singing shores
y lágrimas de monte amanecido	and tears of mountain dawn
en la creciente esfera	in the growing celestial
celeste de su grito.	sphere of its cry.

III   Time and Memory

As an offshoot of the theme of self-encounter, time and memory appear as important considerations in several poems. Memory is often ironic in view of the fact that man learns by experience and must come to terms with the "voice of afterward" which can be a hostile judge, as Don Frontán learned in *Journey*. In the following verses Dieste treats this aspect of self-encounter determined by the passing of time:

Confusa voz tardía,	Confused late voice,
¡desnúdate!	denude yourself!
Voz del después, y nunca	Voice of afterward, and never
del antes, haz presente	of before, make present
una vez tu escondida	for once your hidden
fortaleza.	fortitude.
Quiero contigo un día	One day I want to struggle
combatir en serio	with you seriously
para matarte o para hacerte	to kill you or to make you
mía.	mine.
	(Poem number eleven)

This voice that comes late never quite belongs to us in that it does not spring from our intentions and thus does not influence our actions; it is present only in the act of recalling them.

The encounter with shadows of the past becomes anguished in poems forty and forty-one in which the poet speaks to an impersonal "you" who might be himself or a fellow man such as Don Frontán or Claudio in Dieste's plays:

y si escondido llamas desleal
a memoria que mata, y no es cabal
tu olvido, y te combaten sin figura
recuerdos que no quieren sepultura,
y si te salen sombras al camino
reclamando lugar en tu destino . . .

> and if hidden you call unloyal
> memory that kills, and your forgetfulness
> is not complete, and memories without
> struggle with you not wanting burial,
> and if shadows on your way appear
> demanding a place in your destiny . . .

Almost the whole poem of seven quatrains is one long sentence
presenting a hypothetical struggle with memories which leaves one
neither dead nor alive. The poet concludes: "Y yo te enviaría / mis
águilas después de tu agonía" (And I would send you / my eagles
after your death struggle). A similar conflict appears in the poem
which follows, entitled "En dorado silencio" (In Golden Silence),
urging one to make peace with the dead, confront any last words
spoken in anger, and oblige the offended dead with "claws of love"
to repeat these words until their purest sense emerges. But then,
says the poet, the dead must be left "in golden silence." The
opening verses, with their strange bird image, recall Goya's famous
etching from *The Caprices* entitled "The Dream of Reason Produces
Monsters":

En dorado silencio de sueños olvidados,
allí donde renacen los dioses, la escultura
rota de tus amados muertos deja caer
dulcemente, aunque silben alarma viejos pájaros
dormidos en la infancia de tu miedo

> In golden silence of forgotten dreams
> there where the gods are reborn, let the broken
> sculpture of your beloved dead fall
> sweetly, although old birds may whistle alarm
> asleep in the infancy of your fear.

The soul may descend into the very valley of origin in a sort of
Orphic dream visit to the world of truncated figures which may still
be "sculpted" by the willing visitor, but then the "usual mirror"
should be allowed to return and "the wide river / that unites and

separates shores of desire and memory" be restored.

A number of these previously cited poems may be considered "monodialogues," to use the term coined by Unamuno. This is true also of poem number thirty-nine in which the poet speaks to his youthful self for whom this present moment was once a hopeful future. He asks pardon for having put that youthful heart in danger "by wandering through ambiguous streets of obscure knowledge" and asks him to forget all that may impede his presence in this today that he had once yearned for. In the same way that Dieste's later book *Stories and Inventions of Félix Muriel* recaptures the marvelous childhood vision of life and its promises, the poet here recalls the "simple and lasting essence" of his young self and invokes its presence now:

Tú que no eres pretérito
y quizá fuiste siempre vaticinio,
acepta mi hospedaje sin calcular el mérito
y no sea tu luz lámpara de escrutinio.

You who are not preterite
and perhaps always were promise,
accept my lodging, not calculating merit,
and may your light not be a lamp of scrutiny.

Principio de mi andanza,
vuelve a ser en mi centro dolorido
el que fuiste en figura de encendida esperanza
y funde le reserva en que estás escondido.

Beginning of my journey,
be once more in my aching center
the one you were in a figure of burning hope
and burn out the reserve in which you are hidden.

Memory in these poems of Dieste involves reconciliation with the past, with its shadows sunk in the immobility of death and with one's own self despite the changes wrought by time. Perhaps this reconciliation, present as a problem in Dieste's theater and as an aspiration in his poetry, finds its fullest expression in his prose stories of Félix Muriel.

IV *Human Values and Friendship*

The experiences of self-encounter and of contemplation of the world about us contribute to the poet's vision of life expressed in the following verses:

No me verás ceder a fácil lloro
ni a dulce seducción de sombra mustia,
en que mil soledades hacen coro
sin el decoro de una sola angustia.

You will not see me yield to easy tears
or to the sweet seduction of gloomy shadow,
in which a thousand solitudes echo
without the decorum of one single anguish.

Ni cosechar amor con esa flauta
que muda toda luz en vespertina . . .

Or gather love with that flute
that transforms all light to vespertine . . .

Pues sepa o no mi rumbo, antes soy nauta
sobre desiertos de agua cristalina,
que esa paloma o niño, que amo y ama
con hondura de espejo la onda fina.

For knowing or not my destination, better to be a sailor
On deserts of crystalline water
than that dove or child I love who loves
with mirror depth the slender wave.

Y aun quizá la onda soy—que no reclama
a cambio de caricia golosina.

And even perhaps I am the wave—not demanding
in exchange for affection something sweet to eat.

(Poem forty-three)

The poet characterizes his attitude toward the uncertain life before him. He is not given to melancholy, preferring the decorum of a "single anguish," and though he may not know his destiny, he is no

sadder than a sailor. At the close of the poem he likens himself to a
wave which gives its affection freely.

This spirit of tenderness and of giving is based on the poet's high
regard for human values which also finds expression in poem
seventeen in which he states his concern for people, refusing to pay
homage simply to abstract values:

Si tú no importas, ni yo	If you are not important, or I
ni el otro, ni ese regalo	or the other fellow, or that prize
que espera o que recibió	he expects or received
por ser bueno o por ser malo,	for being good or being bad,
si sólo tiene importancia	if the only important thing is
la Importancia,	Importance,
que venga presto quien diga	let someone come now to say
a qué la importancia obliga	what importance demands
y por qué.	and why.

People, then, are important for our poet and although they are
not subjects of most of his poems they do appear as individuals in
several of them. We have already spoken of Dieste's admiration for
nature's miracles; in poem number thirty-three the wonders of
nature are for sharing. The poet asks his "hidden guest" and
"fugitive guest"—in the final strophe revealed to be the sky—to
remain until his friend arrives. To each stanza of request he adds:
"So that my friend can see you," "I'm going to call my friend," "for
my friend has not arrived yet," "while my friend has not arrived."
Friendship is highly regarded by the poet and in *Stories and
Inventions of Félix Muriel* becomes one of his most esteemed
values.

The poem entitled "Si te hace falta herir" (If You Need to Wound,
22) also treats this important theme but friendship is born of
struggle and striving, not of easy quiescence. It must be worked for
to make the friend's heart "hard and complete" like the poet's own
heart "of shining steel." But as a gesture of true friendship he invites
the other to wound first if he wishes.

"Interior" (2) is a maternal tribute filled with simple and tender
images of light, birds, trees, and the sea which evoke the maternal
voice and face, which then disappear, leaving the son alone hearing
only "the spherical sound / of the bitter sea." Similarly, the father is
recalled in "Perennial Passenger" in the appearance of the son who
seems very much like Don Frontán: "De escondida memoria / vino

a sendas del alba / con ojos andariegos" (From hidden memory / he came on the paths of dawn / with eyes of wandering). Again like Don Frontán, the son can imagine other possibilities "where he could be the father / and the father perhaps a child," but here in contrast the memories are pleasing, recalling paternal affection. The poem speaks of "struggles of wind and songs," of his eyes caressing "shores / of extreme flint," rather crytographic images. The inverted image of the son as father and the father as son recalls Antonio Machado's sonnet "Esta luz de Sevilla" (This Light of Seville) in which the poet calls up the image of his father, still young, looking at him in time and seeing him now with his hair white with age. Dieste, like Machado, explores the intimate galleries of memory and time with the perspicacity of a poet-philosopher. He seems to illustrate perfectly Machado's idea of what the true poet's function is:

El alma del poeta	The poet's soul
se orienta hacia el misterio.	is oriented toward mystery.
Sólo el poeta puede	Only the poet is able
mirar lo que está lejos	to look at what is far
dentro del alma, en turbio	within the soul, wrapped
y mago sol envuelto.	in dark and magic sun.[5]

This is stated in the final verses of Dieste's "Perennial Passenger": "Buscaba el corazón / hacia fuera de sí / cada vez más adentro" (He looked for his heart / outside himself / ever more within).

The subject of love is present in several poems veiled in cryptographic images whose mystery seems to reflect that which lies in each individual. In "Amiga" (Friend in the feminine form, 24) the lovely description of the "desired one" is given in terms of the marvelous and the paradoxical: "dressed and undressed / like a flower, simple array of herself," "near / and far like dawn," and she is seen walking among round rocks on the seashore, attracting silver air about her, leaping over clouds, hermetic yet friendly. While these remarkable qualities are attributed to a very real woman, they are more like those which might describe a view of the moon over a Galician inlet, for as the poet tells us, "of love, sphere and orbit, she is the same." The beautiful and elegant simplicity of the poet's vision of his beloved seen in movement against the nocturnal seascape brings to mind those unforgettable verses of Lord Byron:

> She walks in beauty, like the night
> of cloudless climes and starry skies;
> And all that's best of dark and bright
> Meet in her aspect and her eyes . . .[6]

In the untitled poem which follows "Friend" the poet addresses himself to his beloved in an anxious desire to reach her by "unleashing a fast / gallop of words / which make the heights grow / and shake the plain of my longings." His words and images of earth, sea, and sky are seen as propelled by wings "born from the origin of their accent toward you" but surrender willingly before the impossible quest or disperse like birds, their wings intact. Both poems suggest the paradoxical nature of the beloved as "near and far," "hermetic and friendly," whose inner self cannot be completely discovered even by persistent and impassioned words. Nocturnal seascape again intermingles with a woman's likeness in "Primer viaje por mejillas" (First Journey through Cheeks, 6). Images of clouds, sky, and sea are so intimately joined with the woman in the poet's vision ("the starless night / of your profound tresses") that it is difficult to say whether he describes her cheeks, eyes, eyelids, and hair in terms of nature or whether nature itself is imbued with her human features.

Dieste's poetry in *Loving Red Lantern* may best be described as dense, contrasting somewhat with his prose which tends to be lyrical and expansive. Dieste's verse seems more restrained than his prose, more meditative and intimate. He prefers short-metered verses, particularly octameter in quatrains known as *redondillas*, a traditional popular strophe in the literatures of both Spain and Spanish America. He also uses tercets of eight syllables or less, the sonnet, and the couplet, mixing these and longer strophes with the *redondilla* and generally maintaining rhyme, be it assonant (of vowels) or consonant (of both vowels and consonants). On occasion the longer *alejandrino* form (quatrains of fourteen syllables) may be found, as in the poem "Blasón" (Blazon, 12).

The impression of control, restraint, and economy complements the reflective, and meditative content of the poems. The imagery favors rather simple things with recurrent emphasis on birds, light, riders, mirrors, and marine allusions, but often their references are not transparent but instead suggestive of vague anxieties, doubts, desires, and memories not quite spelled out for the reader. While the images themselves may not be unusual, Dieste combines them in visions of great imaginative force which evoke scenes which one might expect to find in Surrealist painting, as in these verses from "Furia del aire" (Fury of the Air, 45):

Desgarraban el aire florecillas de vidrio
y el aire se encarama en el árbol más alto
y busca el horizonte
no queriendo saber que su pecho ¡tan claro!
está negro y herido.
. . .
A la nube más blanca rompió el calabrote
de pasmo que sujeta las nubes a los montes
y se hizo huracán
por huir de sí mismo.

      Little flowers of glass were tearing the air
      and the air climbs up on the highest tree
      and seeks the horizon
      not wanting to know that its breast, so clear!
      is black and wounded.
      . . .
      Of the whitest cloud it broke the cabled rope
      of wonder which subjects the clouds to the mountains
      and turns into a hurricane
      to flee from itself.

Much more than a mere scene, however, what Dieste presents is a veritable drama of nature in which his experience in writing for the theater may be noted. Theater imagery is present in the poem "Eco" (Echo, 21), as well as the mirror motif which is so important in his other writings:

actor sin gesto, ni figura,
ni escenario;

pariente de fantasmas
y de espejos cansados;

espejo de sí mismo
y a sí mismo se dobla,
y, en repetido salto,
con la sonora presa
huye agonizando;

actor without gesture, or form
or stage;

relative of ghosts
and of tired mirrors;

mirror of itself
that duplicates itself,
and, in a repeated leap,
with the resounding prey
flees while dying;

The echo is represented by several metaphors of a static nature, and then as part of a dramatic scene as the final agony of someone "dead who is dying, / for in death there are degrees." It is also a "heart startled with another's beats." The final verses surprisingly and dramatically transfer the audible sounds of the echo to the inaudible interior world of the poet's (or perhaps someone else's) anguish and desolation which now may be seen as the inspiration for the somber images of death, pallor, and emptiness: " el eco / repetía el agudo / silencio de tu llanto" (the echo / was repeating the sharp / silence of your weeping). As in other poems in this volume, an outside reality is translated into poetic imagery which achieves the expression of interior or intimate reality.

Surely it is our author's propensity for Surrealist imagery that prompted Mariano Gómez to say the following in his poem of tribute which introduces the volume:

Carne azul de la vida,	Blue flesh of life,
lo mejor de los sueños	the best of dreams
sueña en tu poesía.	dreams in your poetry.

A sí mismos los sueños	Dreams meditate upon
soñando se meditan	themselves by dreaming
y el pensamiento nace	and thought grows
en la luz siempre viva.	in the ever-glowing light.

There is also Surrealist suggestion in the blending of opposites, recalling André Breton's conception of the optimum point of Surrealism in which opposites cease to be perceived as such. This is particularly common in Dieste's rendering of nature, "river in the sky, rain" (44), "the sea-green sun" (3), and:

Cielo como el agua	Sky like water
y agua de cielos caídos	and water of fallen skies
allá en el principio.	there in the beginning.
El día y la noche son alba.	Day and night are dawn.

. . .   . . .

Como en cielo, el árbol
en agua tan vivo.
Son nubes las algas y algas las nubes
entotal ensueño: celeste y marino

As in sky, the tree
in water so alive.
The seaweed are clouds and clouds seaweed
in total dream: celestial and marine.
("Ribera" [Shore], 46)

Naturally this blending is inspired by the elements themselves, in
the similar expanses of ocean and of sky whose point of meeting
cannot be distinguished by the eye, but Dieste carries the visual
stimulus even further, and in the same poem presents a Surrealist
vision of metamorphosis and spontaneous verbal suggestion:

Las palabras nacen, respiran,
son flores diciéndose, labios
floreciendo, gritos
que vuelan y nadan, mordiscos
del alma en la fruta del cielo íntegro

Words are born, they breathe,
are flowers saying themselves, lips
that flower, cries
that fly and swim, bites
of the soul in the fruit of the whole sky

Another characteristic of a number of poems is baroque language
and structure which lend a tone of complex reflection reminiscent of
Golden Age poetry in the same way that Dieste's plays convey an
atmosphere of classical Spanish theater. There are echoes of
conceptismo (conceptism) in word play, yet the poet's verbal
complexities are not essentially decorative, but used to achieve
ingenious conciseness, subtlety, and stimulation of thought. The
philosophical sonnet twenty-nine offers an example in its first
stanza:

Si entre ser y decir hay preferir
al más alto decir prefiero el ser
y antes morir arriesgo que exponer
el ser a ser no ser en el decir.

If between being and saying there be preference
to the highest saying I prefer being
and sooner death would risk than expose
the being to not being in saying.

These verses, with their apparent contradiction and word play ponder the power of speech which is capable of conceiving and declaring the possibility of not being, that is to say, of negating itself. Dieste's conceptist handling of the power of speech as a manifestation of thought capable of casting doubt on the reality of existence has all the profundity of Calderón de la Barca's conceptist poetry in his famous *La vida es sueño* (Life Is a Dream). The conceptism is not simply for sport or for acoustic decoration; it lends a classical elegance and conciseness which invites the reader to meditate and ponder difficult and paradoxical concepts.

The contemplation of what might bring death, and so silence the poet's voice gives rise to conceptist verses in which the baroque manipulation of words conveys most effectively the ambiguous, uncertain nature of death:

Si algo, más y menos   If something, more and less
algo que cualquier algo,   something than just any something,
y más flor que esa flor   and more of a flower than that flower
sepultada en hallazgo   buried in discovery
. . .   . . .
si algo así y no así,   if something like that and not like that,
con sus alas tan leves   with its wings so light
esta mi voz segara   this, my voice, should cut down

(Poem forty-nine)

In addition to play on words inspired by concepts, these verses and many others show another baroque characteristic, the inversion of word order combined with postponed subjects, verbs, or conclusions. In poem forty, for example, the first four stanzas present hypothetical conditions while the conclusion is delayed to a much later point in the poem. Inversion of natural word order is very apparent in the baroque sonnet previously cited: "No tanto sino más, enmudecer / es para el alma espanto que morir" (Not equally, but more, silence / is for the soul frightful than dying, 29). A more normal word order might be: Silence is not equally but more frightful for the soul than dying. Even allowing for natural differences between Spanish and English word order and for a reasonable degree of poetic inversion, the alteration of logical sequence in this and other poems is so pronounced that it requires careful reflection, which may very well be what the author intended.

The persistence of the color green is to be noted in several poems: "green night" (27), "green spherical light" (38), "the green sea of my fluid dreams" (48), "green tumult of the solitary sea" (8), "green wonder" of a river (44), "green fangs of dogs" (42), and "sea-green sun" (3). While the color seems to be associated with the sea, it is applied to other objects and sensations with a dreamlike recurrence.

Even after pointing out these distinctive qualities of Dieste's verse, it remains difficult to categorize them because of the great variation in meter, form, imagery, and ideas. It may be said that he follows the *ars poetica* of "The Miller's Surprise" in that the mill or poetic form is not unusual, but the water he channels within its limits creates signs, fancies, and dramas unforeseen perhaps even by the artist himself.

One might wonder why Dieste never published another book of poetry after *Loving Red Lantern*, especially since it was so well received by the critics. The pronounced lyricism of the prose found in *Stories and Inventions of Félix Muriel* would seem to suggest that his creativity preferred a less restrictive mill in which to channel itself so that it is free to meander without the restraints of meter, rhyme, and the measured pauses which are present even in free verse.

CHAPTER 7

The Memorable World of Félix Muriel

IT is ironic that a book hailed in 1974 as "perhaps the finest book of
stories of our century in the Spanish language" had been
virtually unknown in Spain for over three decades.[1] The first edition
of *Historias e invenciones de Félix Muriel* (Stories and Inventions of
Felix Muriel), published in 1943 in Buenos Aires with beautiful
illustrations by Luis Seoane, was greeted with enthusiasm in
Argentina and Uruguay, but it was not until 1974, when the volume
was reedited in Madrid, that it was accorded the unequivocable
recognition that it deserves as one of the most extraordinary books
of Spanish fiction of our times.

Many critics have pointed out the book's magical or poetic
realism, lyrical prose, and exploration of memory, but they have
generally avoided exegesis and analysis, directing their attention to
the rediscovery of Dieste and his incorporation into the mainstream
of twentieth-century Spanish literature, and rightly so, in view of
his long absence from the peninsular literary scene. In a way, the
critics' treatment of *Félix Muriel* is like what happens in the story
"El jardín de Plinio" (Pliny's Garden) when the professor Don
Julián, interested in hearing Félix's interpretation, asks him if he
likes to listen to dreams. Félix responds affirmatively and listens
attentively but refrains from offering any conjecture, so the reader
in turn is left to venture his own ideas. Indeed the magic of these
stories may be broken when rendered into paraphrase much as a
dream resists expository analysis if it is to retain its mystery;
nevertheless, it is only through serious examination that Dieste's
creativeness can be fully appreciated. The book does not easily fall
into the usual terms used to designate genre. It has been called a
novel, reflections, a poem and even a literary fugue. Pere Gimferrer
views it as "an atomized novel" and a "fragmentary and divided
biography"; Dámaso Santos as "a poetic novel"; and José Marra-
López as "a strange and prodigious book of stories . . . marginal to
all possible classifications."[2]

Through the eyes and ears of Félix Muriel we are admitted to the wonders that lie latent and often undiscovered in the familiar world around us. The magical vision of Félix focuses on his past in a Galician setting totally foreign to concrete historical fact. References to the Spanish Civil War, present to some degree or disguised in most of Dieste's contemporaries, are notably absent. While echoes of Spain's cataclysmic fraternal strife were still very much alive when *Félix Muriel* was published, their absence in the book does not represent evasion, for the reflective and contemplative exercise of memory here is not a gratuitous recovery of things past but rather a quest for answers of great consequence. There are philosophical questions, a search for self-knowledge, and a call for compassion and recognition of responsibility which are at the heart of postwar thought. In the Galician setting of these stories, Dieste also effects a vicarious return to his native region and to a recent past which often seems as remote as the ancient myths. Such an examination of the past by means of fantasy, memory, and writing as a search for meaning, knowledge, and self-understanding cannot be said to evade reality but rather to transcend it.

I *"The Cherry-colored Oil Lamp"*

"El quinqué color guinda," a lovely vignette written in poetic prose, serves as portico to the selections which follow just as the lamp recalled by the narrator illuminated the landing where greetings and good-byes were exchanged, which was his portico to life. The past is evoked by recalling the cherry-colored oil lamp which becomes a sort of magical mirror or crystal ball to the child's eyes. Twice the narrator repeats that "great familiarity and vast mystery" were ensconced in the lamp, which witnessed the daily affairs of the household and at the same time emitted mysterious promises:

Great promises are made in a thousand ways; they travel in the clouds, they are horses' manes, or suddenly they are caged like a small sun bird in a glass of water . . . in the cherry color of an oil lamp, without anyone's knowing it other than one, the child who looks at it (12).

The lamp is associated with the voices of family friends and the cherry color with a "liquor of friendship which is never consumed" (12).

In the alchemy of the child's fantasy, water and fire join to create the marvel of reflecting everyday reality and a dreamworld:

And I who came running and approached its illuminated solitude, am sure of having seen there within it populous cities in which a child may get lost, until one joins the melted crystal of its pools and the dense fire of its lights (13).

The oil lamp, constant in its place while family life carries on and changes, is like a sun illuminating the child's universe, the stairs and landing which provide his first metaphysical experiences. There he learns to appreciate space, angles, and infinity in a microcosm which produces notions of eternity transcending time.

Dieste translates the enchantment of the child's experiences into lovely poetic images, some highly visual, as a glass "lightly modulated like a small ocean in which twilight was rocking" (11), or a smile "like a little piece of lemon" (12). A deaf friend of the family makes the sensitive child aware of a world unhindered by sound; "how nice to be deaf like Doña María" (12). There is a pervading tone of sadness in the use of the past tense that relegates the marvelous lamp presiding over the childhood universe to an age long past. The lamp which brought him dreams of faraway places and notions of familiar reality can only be recreated by the equally magical lamp of memory.

II *"This Child is Crazy"*

In "Este niño está loco," the narrator recalls swimming on his father's back and the thrill of flying a kite with his father, a powerful man who knew how to deal with the elements. Their house, "deep rather than large, and though very bright and not at all labyrinthine, full of tranquil and exemplary mystery" (19), has a parlor which particularly fascinates him with its grave darkness and pictures of grandparents now gone, who look at him as if they remember him. It also has a mirror in which reality is reflected silently with three harmless dragons imprisoned under a marble top upon which a crystal clock and a music box rest. He considers being sent to the parlor to get something as a feat testing his worthiness. One "night of great darkness" after visitors have left and everyone is busy in silent labor, he watches his father enter and leave the dark parlor, never quite coming into the bright light of the dining room and looking at him in a strange way. In one of those "dawns, coming from there, from the profound night of the ancestors and of the mirror, it seemed to me that he had many stars clinging to his chest and beard" (20). His father advances, perhaps half in jest at a sort of processional pace as if trying to impress his smallest son, to "surprise and maybe scare him a little" (20). Sensing something secret, the child imitates his father by venturing into the dark parlor and staying there after his father leaves. A playful but imperious call sends Félix running out of the room in rapid flight till he feels the protective hand of his father on his head.

The "adventure" is basically one which universally causes fright in children—entering a dark room (recalling Dieste's early Galician story "Children's Fright"). It becomes an awesome, traumatic adventure, and beyond that, a metaphysical experience in which the young Félix ventures into a land of darkness, silence, death, and the past, from which he is allowed to return to the comforting realm of life and light. The interior drama is very vividly communicated by a carefully delineated process of mythification. His father, white-bearded "friend of a capricious sea," is compared to Neptune with a child on his back. Aloft, the kite's triumph over the air and the earth convinces the imaginative child that his father has a special way of communicating with the powerful elements, "Yes, he knew. He had great friends with whom he shared the world's secrets" (18). Like the peaks of Barbanza, "a great power thickened into gentleness," his father seems a powerful yet gentle challenger of mysteries. Félix has a special gift for perceiving the marvelous quality of familiar objects, such as the "thousand clear or terrible skies that make the house travel or suddenly leave it anchored in the mirror of its former days" (18). It is this extraordinary ability to turn the commonplace into the transcendental which makes his trip into the dark parlor an Orphic visit to the netherworld, Hades in miniature. The parlor has several attributes which liken it to a shadowy underworld. The portraits of the ancestors seem to draw Félix into a land of things past while the mirror reflects scenes in a weird, silent way so that he sees visitors "with their same gestures, their same pale hands, but without voices and without that light noise the fans made opening and closing" (19). This is the silent abode of death, guarded by three dragons, much less intimidating than the darkness, like figures from the netherworld whose original plan was forgotten. Félix realizes his father "knew how to go into the deepest ancestral night, in whose bosom one is born, though it seems also

that of death" (20). Mythological implications are underscored by
the music Félix's sister has been playing, "Gradus ad Parnassum"
(Trip to Parnassus, abode of the Greek god Apollo and the muses).
The child's hurried return is less dignified than his father's ritual
pace, but no matter, for he emerges from the Orphic trial victorious
on that unforgettable "night of great silence in the whole house, the
whole town, I think in the whole world" (18).

One feels the tremendous sensitivity not only of Félix but also of
his father who seems to guess that their "game" is a good deal more
than that. He seems concerned when he is unable to see his child
who has stayed behind. An insensitive observer might well think,
like Aunt Eulalia, that Félix is crazy, but only because not everyone
can perceive the marvelous quality the child confers upon his
accomplishment.

In Lewis Carroll's classic, *Alice In Wonderland*, Alice enters a
dreamland of unreality inhabited by strange and fanciful creatures.
The wonderland of Félix Muriel, on the other hand, is his own very
familiar world transformed into a place of marvels by his poetic
imagination. Dieste's story proves that fiction does not have to
portray the unusual to be exciting; all that is needed is the
imaginative childlike vision of Félix Muriel. The effect of great
silence is enhanced by the fact that absolutely no dialogue occurs in
the story until the closing comment of Aunt Eulalia which serves to
break the spell. The silence makes the visual effects particularly
impressive, as when the child sees his father with stars adorning his
beard and chest. "This Child Is Crazy" is one of Dieste's most
beautiful stories, turning a child's natural admiration for his father
and fear of the dark into a metaphysical adventure of mythological
proportions never to be forgotten.

III *"Juana Rial, Flowering Lemon Tree"*

In the story "Juana Rial, limonero Florido," the narrator recalls a
clear day a few years before when a faraway memory came to him of
an old woman who lived in complete isolation in a tiny broken-down
house, inviting the hostility of the townspeople who consider her a
sinister witch. Somber, cursing, and totally alone, she is the town
scapegoat, especially when poor fishing and bad times inspire the
collective stoning of her house. The beseiged woman, hit in the
forehead by a stone, cries out: "My name is Juana Rial, of good
family and upbringing. I was thrown into the world; to this garden I

came. Damn! Damn! You will all see me at the foot of your beds!"
(28). Having lost their common enemy, the townspeople are
dispersed by deep sorrow about to stir hostility among them. The
narrator, though a small child then,

> participated in the invasion with as much heroism as the rest and equal
> curiosity that was uncontrollable because we had all fantasied a lot about
> that darkness observed by cobwebs and perhaps we had thrown our stones
> with such rage to penetrate its secret (28).

The young narrator, however, stays behind, noting pictures of a
boat and a sailor in the bare house. Looking out at the familiar
waves, he is disturbed at the strangeness of their sounds, likening
the sensation to touching the stalks from which the great straw
giants of the fair are made. Feeling the ocean's eyes on him, he
manages enough courage to touch the victim's forehead and,
frightened by the cold and by the "impossible sea" leaves in great
haste.

The remoteness of this strange memory, which has stamped itself
all too vividly on the narrator's mind, is recreated by the baroque
setting of a story in a frame within a frame. The narrator does not
recall the experience directly, but rather by recalling another day a
few years before, similar to the day he tells us about in the story he
remembers. He teases the reader enough to awaken his curiosity by
saying that the story is not particularly important and that he is
almost sorry for mentioning it on seeing us so serious. As in other
Dieste fiction, light and dark are effectively used to create and
dispel mystery. The narrator realizes now that he knew "little more
of her than that sad ray which resounds an instant among the roof
tiles of a small church at the hour when no one is there." It is
stressed that the old lady's house is closed to all light except for a red
candle seen at night, a sure sign that she is involved in conjuration
and the devil's work.

The presentation of the story as a childhood memory makes it
possible for the narrator to reflect upon the experience, extract its
deepest implications a posteriori, and imbue it with the lyrical
intensity only an adult writer can provide. The child's reaction was
instinctively profound but the adult perspective illuminates the
experience. The narrator can now offer human motives for the old
lady's receiving and advising strangers as her probable need for
communication, and money, and as nostalgia for love. His remain-

ing in the house led him to discover that the reputed witch was nothing more than a "poor creature," a miserable human being rejected by life, love, fortune, people, and death itself, for even the cypress trees associated with cemeteries and death "guarded the chastity of death with more invulnerable ceremony" (27) when she passed by.

There is great irony in the hyperbole which characterizes the attack on the helpless old woman as a heroic "invasion." When the child stays inside her house and looks out, his perspective changes. It is a solemn and prodigious moment in which he learns what it is like to be utterly alone and ostracized. The lyrical cadence reflects the rhythm of the waves now impersonal and strange:

I had seen the sea and the sky and I had seen the gulls and the eyes of an ox. I had seen those great dazzling waves. I had seen them, but now they were looking at me, one after the other, one after the other, huge, raising themselves, singing (29).

Like the straw giants whose imposing mystery is broken by touching the humble materials of their manufacture, the legends and fantasies about the town witch vanish with proximity and the child experiences a moment of solitary communion before the sea and his conscience.

The strange discourse of the dying woman, reconstructed by the memory of the townspeople and the narrator, explains somewhat their feelings of guilt which emerge as hostility against each other and in attributing her death to fear, hunger, or old age. The witch identifies herself by name and, with the disappearance of anonymity, she becomes a specific human being of good family, victim of misfortune and a flowering lemon tree in a hostile orchard. The lemon suggests her bitterness, like that of the fruit produced by the plant after flowering. We realize too that her defensive solitude has been drawn about her like the abundant thorns of the lemon tree which repel all who would come close. Her final curse is not so much that of a witch as that of a poor creature whose death will forever haunt the "heroic" invaders, as indeed it continues to haunt the memory of the narrator so many years later.

IV   *"The Stuffed Parrot"*

There was, Félix Muriel tells us in "El loro disecado," a parrot chained in the store of Naval Supplies and Related Items owned by

Don Ramón. It looked so lifelike that people spoke to it, but Don Ramón insisted that the parrot was thinking and remembering, "he has a right to his silence" (33). At home Félix's father would repeat some of the anecdotes involving the parrot and animated conversations about sailing and the sea, in particular a discussion between Don Ramón and Lisardito, a pharmacy student and philosopher who thinks the world is too small for man. Don Ramón jovially defends his views, insisting that "there's a right to deafness, gentlemen" (35). The young Félix was sometimes allowed to accompany his father to Don Ramón's store where he heard fragments of mysterious stories about olden days. One night in the empty store Félix is given some picture books to read while his father and Don Ramón converse after midnight near the door. He tries hard not to listen; "Maybe for that reason I heard everything with surprising clarity" (38). When Don Ramón is convinced that Félix is absorbed in his books, he begins his story which "went toward the sidewalk, stopped in the middle of the store, submerged itself in the darkness of the hall, and finally became hushed in the most exciting part of the story, since both sat down again" (40).

Don Ramón tells Muriel that he couldn't keep his promise to "her" or write during the two years he was away from Amberes. He refers rather ambiguously to a man and a beautiful woman with a lovely voice. They weren't married but like a ferocious and jealous tyrant he kept her with him. She was not a coquette but was waiting for a love which might redeem her from fear of him. Two years later, a friend who arrived earlier at Amberes informs him that he found the old hotel abandoned except for a familiar voice inviting him to enter, which turned out to be a parrot's voice. A man in mourning explained to him that the hotel was closed since his wife's death but that the door was left open because he is expecting someone. Don Ramón somehow finds himself at the door of the hotel and realizes that the man is waiting for him. The other announces almost with pleasure that the woman is dead, and then treacherously attacks Don Ramón with a knife. Don Ramón, however, is prepared and kills him first. Suddenly the parrot says: *"merci beaucoup"* (thank you very much, in French) in the dead woman's voice. Unable to bear this phrase in constant repetition, the exasperated sailor shoots the parrot with a pellet gun on board his ship and has it stuffed.

Don Ramón realizes Félix has been listening. The boy's father takes leave of his friend with unaccustomed affection and instead of walking directly home with Félix, takes him in silence far from town and asks him if he is afraid. Félix answers that he is not, with him there. And alone?, his father insists. "We'll see," answers the child. Then they talk about hearing Don Ramón's story and Félix promises, "I won't say anything." Then for the first time his father shakes his hand as if with an adult, as he had done with Don Ramón. The story is told rather simply, leaving the reader to penetrate its mysteries, ambiguities, and omissions such as the exact relationship between the woman and the hotel keeper, how Don Ramón and the woman were able to communicate, and precisely how she died. The man simply announces, "Elle est morte" (She is dead), which Don Ramón interprets as meaning, "I killed her. She is an exclusive possession" (43).

The baroque structure of Dieste's story submerges us deeper and deeper into the world of Félix Muriel, with multiple stories within stories. First there is the narrative of Félix in which his father's stories are reproduced and then Don Ramón's story which contains that of his friend who had returned to Amberes before he did. The invention imparts a strong impression of grotesqueness. Early in the story we see the school mistress's mother who "looked like a little parrot" trying to induce the reticent parrot to speak, until she is shocked to learn that it is stuffed. The bizarre couple in Amberes is like Beauty and the Beast, with the man described as having little eyes, thin lips, and white shaven hair. Don Ramón cites the thank you uttered by the parrot as the most grotesque experience of his life. The incongruity of Félix's impulse to laugh while Don Ramón turns livid is also grotesque as is the presence of the stuffed bird during the conversation between Muriel and Don Ramón.

As is common in Dieste's fiction, "reality" is reflected in several ways. A mirrored view of the hotel keeper reveals his ferocious nature. The parrot's voice is an imitation reflecting the dead woman's voice with deceptive fidelity. Other ways of mirroring events are memory and narrative. Don Ramón tries to kill a live memory by shooting the parrot, but like the stuffed bird which is chained though it obviously cannot escape, Don Ramón is chained to the past by memory, "I remembered her during the two years I was away and continue to remember her though she doesn't hold a candle to my wife" (40). He achieves some measure of liberation by confessing to his trusted friend. There is, as he says, a right to silence, but also a need to communicate when secrets "begin to be an obstacle" (38).

Telling a secret and hearing one imply certain mutual obligations, however, for Don Ramón cites two rights, silence and deafness.

Although he seems on the verge of telling his story to Lisardito, he obviously does not feel the latter can handle it. He says in nautical terms that if Lisardito is overloaded, he will fling the cargo overboard before sinking (38). Don Ramón cannot tell his wife either because he does not want her to have to bear such a burden. Muriel has the option of not listening to his friend's story but decides to hear it if it will be of help. Félix unwittingly becomes part of the secret and is impressed when his father treats him as an equal, capable of knowing the truth without losing his esteem for Don Ramón and without telling anyone. There is, however, a certain irony in Félix's telling the story to us, as if he too feels the need to relieve the weight of the confession years later when it seems far away and cannot harm his father's friend. As in "This Child Is Crazy," there seems to be a very special sensitivity shared by Félix and his father. We also see the boy from his father's point of view when he tells Don Ramón that he reads a lot, is pretty bright, not malicious, and has an extraordinary memory for recalling events, but not for running errands.

Don Ramón's story only occupies about half of Felix's narration. The first part, a sort of introduction which establishes the themes of one's right to silence and also not to listen, prepares us for the story about the acquisition of the parrot, which we first expect Don Ramón to tell Lisardito, but which is postponed until he confides to Muriel. The grotesque story contrasts with the animated banter of the introduction, which contains details that in retrospect may be seen as contributing symbolically to the anecdote that follows. Don Ramón, for example, recommends that Félix peruse the *Nautical Guide*, for "one must learn to tie and untie" (38), a lesson applicable to experiences in life. Félix's surprise in reading that the most beautiful mushrooms are poisonous anticipates his surprise in learning that the gregarious Don Ramón holds a dark secret within him. Muriel, suspecting that his son will regard his old friend with fear and mistrust, teaches the boy to carry the burdens of others with respect and dignity. Thus Félix learns that even those who seem transparent and familiar may hold great secrets in the same way as the cherry-colored oil lamp in the first story reflects "great familiarity and vast mystery."

V *"Pliny's Garden"*

Pliny's garden, "El jardín de Plinio," is a run-down patio alongside a boarding house where the student Félix Muriel and the history professor Don Julián live. The professor is given a dog named Pliny whom he sets up in the garden filled with sundry items discarded by the tenants. As Don Julián meditates about this garden which is like Limbo and about his own life—a story in pieces to be put together—he sees Félix Muriel throw a bundle of papers into Limbo, and his archeological calling makes him feel responsible for piecing the papers together. The manuscript Don Julián retrieves is an unfinished novel about an unnamed protagonist who "like many others, had lost his memory" (53) but was fully aware of having lost it. His friend, with whom he discusses the problem in Socratic dialogue, later loses his understanding but abandons the search to go into business. The professor continues picking up discarded sheets until he finds one with the word "etcetera." He returns it to Félix Muriel who ponders, "one keeps leaving so many etceteras behind, that recovering one . . ." (58). Don Julián reminds him that they may eventually lead to finding something. The following scene shows Don Julián before his class, going back to lesson one instead of continuing with the fifteenth lesson as planned. He confesses his disillusion with history which in its pure form is an inevitable and impersonal testimony of arbitrary events, a completely inert and terrible etcetera.

Canel, another student boarder, adds a hedgehog to Pliny's garden. Instead of becoming accustomed to the spiny animal, the dog seems to go crazy. The professor confides to Félix Muriel a dream in which he is in Pliny's place. Pliny becomes sad, wan, and retiring, so Canel offers to take the hedgehog away but Don Julián declines, seeking a natural and judicious solution. He equates the hedgehog with the volcano Vesuvius whose eruption killed the dog's namesake, the Roman historian Pliny. Inspired by that event and by his dream, Don Julián decides to remove Pliny, with Félix's complicity, to a place free from danger. In the closing scene they hear a shot as Pliny participates in a hunt, and both the professor and Félix claim responsibility. "It was a fresh and very beautiful morning that the author or witness of this story will always remember" (74).

A central question arising from the story is that of man's inquiring nature, his efforts to see and understand the world about him and himself. This may be seen on several levels. On the most elementary plane is the curiosity of the dog who explores the objects he finds but makes no decisions. As an innocent animal he chews an old shoe or a young student's manuscript with equal satisfaction.

The child Faustinito, the landlady's son, learns not only by touching but also by questioning: Is Limbo the same as Imbo? Is a hedgehog edible? On a higher level, the protagonist of Félix's manuscript—obviously his alter ego—engages in sophisms with his friend in search of his lost memory. The professor is not satisfied with what the academic exercise of his discipline teaches him about history:

And what does Homo sapiens know about Canis vulgaris and vice versa? And in turn what does Homo sapiens know about Homo sapiens and vice versa? Man, man, I know very little about you, even less about myself, and believe me, it is little! And vice versa? You about me? (57).

His students, dependent upon a textbook and professor for their knowledge of history, know even less, for which reason Don Julián imagines that they have their backs turned to him even when they are facing him.

The theme is foreshadowed in the very first paragraph of the story in which the honeysuckles "scaled the wall to see a little horizon and with their light aroma and happy trembling to reach the top and faint on the other side" (49), imitating man's aspiration to see more of the world even if the effort is fatal. Dieste's story reveals the need for empirical knowledge, its frustrations and its dangers, illustrated by the Roman historian's fatal insistence on observing Vesuvius firsthand. He uses the technique of demythifying history for the purpose of translating it into terms of familiar and even trivial experience to make "inert history" live for the individual. Thus in this account containing "events of indubitable importance" (62), the famous historian Pliny the Elder (23 A.D. to 79 A.D.) is demythified in the canine Pliny who is as attracted by the mystery of the hedgehog as the other by that of Vesuvius but is saved from danger by Don Julián. The latter, however, is another Pliny who envies the way his dog examines every object he encounters in the garden. He intuitively associates himself with the dog Pliny in the dream he recounts to Félix Muriel in which he is housed in a large trunk-house and flings a vast array of sundry objects from his suitcases out to the sea.

His search for real knowledge in the midst of academia brings him to question the value of his lifelong dedication to his studies. After confessing his doubts to his students, he tells them to forget everything he has said until they learn by their own experience, as he himself will continue to do, though it be dangerous. Others are less tenacious, as the friend in Félix's novel who abandons the pursuit of understanding and becomes a successful businessman. The dangers of direct experience are also expressed in the scene in which Faustinito inquires about the contents of a test tube in Canel's room and the student admonishes, "Don't touch, for fear of death" (67). The name Faustinito in itself demythifies the literary hero whose desire for knowledge in Goethe's famous work led to a pact with the devil which posed mortal danger for his soul.

Another demythified concept is that of Limbo, the abode of the dead whose souls, though free of personal sin, are denied the beatitude of heaven. Here it is a place for things which have no place, where articles are strewn into the void and come to rest before the curiosity of a dog and his master. The garden of the title may be seen as an ironical allusion to that of Eden from which Adam and Eve were expelled because of their curiosity in eating of the tree of knowledge. Pliny's expulsion from his innocent state and his transformation into a hunter would suggest a parody of this biblical episode.

The themes of history and memory are interrelated in the story, since memory is a form of reproducing history, which is seen by the professor as a monstrous etcetera inexorably registering man's achievements and destructions without ever being destroyed itself. As long as history or "inert memory" is not perceived as vital experience, it is nothing more than a series of impersonal etceteras, an inevitable succession of variable events. It simply requires that something—anything—happen, and even destructions are indestructible insofar as they continue being history. These considerations lead Don Julián and Félix Muriel to resolve together to destroy the papers the latter had thrown from his window and the former had carefully reconstructed, thus liberating themselves from the tyranny of history.

Also affecting the pursuit of knowledge is the problem of language, which may hinder understanding. Don Julian's "Limbo" and Faustinito's erroneous "Imbo" both suggest to them the same sensation of emptiness on a nonverbal level. Terminology often depends on point of view, as when Faustinito calls an "illustrious species" of beetle a dried cockroach and asks if the hedgehog sticks or the victim is stuck. The very first sentence of the story suggests shades of meaning which make communication difficult, "that could be, according to the way one looked at it, a little run-down garden, a yard aspiring to be a garden, or perhaps a patio with a certain vocation for becoming a yard" (49). Pliny's abode is a trunk-house, akin to Don Quijote's famous *baciyelmo* or shaving dish-helmet, its reality determined as much by its current use as by its original intention.

Another difficulty in acquiring knowledge is that of relating and synthesizing the multitudinous elements which enter our experience like the discarded objects thrown into Pliny's garden. The archeological calling of Don Julián reveals itself in his obsession to piece together Félix Muriel's manuscript. His pedagogical method is that of digression around the theme of the lesson until it is seen from several angles. The structure of Dieste's story in fact reflects this multiperspective approach. The description of the garden, Pliny's encounter with the enigmatic hedgehog, Félix's unfinished novel, Don Julián's lecture and dream, Faustinito's questions, and conversations between Don Julián and Félix are the diverse elements the reader must piece together and try to interpret.

Themes of great importance such as knowledge, history, and fraternity are presented in terms of everyday trivial experience, for it is only in individual experience that the diverse etceteras of history derive the dynamism of "live memory." The individual, Don Julián, can save the innocent Pliny from the hedgehog by making what he terms a "juridical" decision. It should be noted that in Spanish the word *historia* means both collective history and story, in the sense of literary fiction. Thus the considerations about history arising from Dieste's story may be taken to include apocryphal history or stories which communicate experience on a personal level which Miguel de Unamuno preferred to call "intrahistory."

Friendship is seen as something which can help alleviate the anxieties of man's limited cognition. Don Julián comes to respect his young friend Félix Muriel and they share together the responsibility for destroying the manuscript and for removing Pliny. The professor says that blank papers are nothing, "but with a little adjustment in the end can be the bridge to finding something" (58). Perhaps that something may be nothing more than sharing anxieties, for when he asks, "Does a poet always know what he is doing with what he says, no matter how well he knows what he says?" (63), Félix responds, "He knows at least what he wants to do. Delve into brotherhood, to make it true or end it." They seal their friendship by "the extremely serious task" of tearing the manuscript into smaller pieces that a light wind carries away.

"Pliny's Garden" is the second longest story in the book and occupies the very center, acting as a sort of axis containing a philosophical and aesthetical statement. Writing novels, like registering historical data, involves the selection of possible events. Don Julián asks, "Of what importance is this event or another with its successive connection?" (60). On a personal level, Don Julián contemplates his life as a story in pieces to be put together and Félix's manuscript as another story in fragments. Their aspirations are very similar: to coordinate the pieces by means of reflection, to vitalize them by memory, and to acquire a consciousness of what otherwise is a mere succession of events. To remember and to reflect is to find meaning, with the help of empirical experience, fantasy, dreams, fable, and friendship. Conversations like those of Félix and Don Julián provide not only visions of the other person but also of ourselves as others view us. One becomes accustomed to some things, but the mystery of man and self can be as exasperating for people like Félix Muriel and Don Julián as the enigmatic hedgehog for Pliny the dog and the volcano for Pliny the Elder.

VI *"The Blank Book"*

In an almost facetious tone, the story "El libro en blanco" introduces an old man who "was a saint and no one knew it" (77), including himself. He occupies himself in tasks boring to younger people, like shelling beans, while he watches the distant valley and recalls the past. Suddenly the shadow by which he judges the time seems to grow and a stranger carrying an enormous book asks for some water. After drinking he throws the glass into the air and it lands on the window sill unbroken. The old man asks the stranger if he lives by such tricks, and the latter's answer that it is two questions—whether he lives and whether it be by such tricks— leads to a conversation in which the old man shows surprising cleverness in countering the rather enigmatic comments of the other. The mysterious stranger says that magic is his way of cursing and laughing at patience, work, and the stars which the old man admires. He then identifies himself as the devil who carries the book of humanity's sins and, pointing to the page where those of the village are registered, invites him to add further accusations of the villagers derived from his personal experience and long memory. Not finding his own name there, the old peasant writes it on a blank page, inventing terrible sins to make those of the village seem fewer. He proceeds to cross out sins from the records of people he knows and looks up to find the visitor gone and the book completely blank.

This is obviously one of Félix Muriel's "inventions," a variation on the traditional folktale involving the devil, for as the old man comments, "Times change and don't change, depending" (78). As in most folklore encounters between the devil and human beings, the devil tries to tempt the man's pride, but we realize at the end that the old peasant's humility has triumphed and his kindness has redeemed others less saintly than he. The old man's saintliness is also suggested in subtle details such as his childlike wonder at the things of nature, his concern for a little boy he observes from afar, and in his affection for animals reminiscent of Saint Francis of Assisi. He can recall all the animals he has had since childhood, their names, peculiarities, and days spent in their company, showing the same prodigious memory which would have facilitated his complying with the devil's request.

Ironically the peasant who asks himself "why should an old man be useless even though he might be a useless old man" turns out to be the most useful person in the village. For all his supposed lack of urbanity and professed lack of education, he is far more clever and urbane than his visitor. When the devil insists that he has asked him two questions instead of one, the peasant shows great sagacity when he says that one question can indeed be two in the same manner as a stick cut in two may be two sticks, but an ear of corn cut in half does not form two ears. The peasant's retorts repeatedly leave the devil so disconcerted that his only recourse is to resort to magic tricks.

An important theme in the tale is that of magic, miracles, and the marvelous. The courteous old man manifests a reasonable amount of interest in the devil's "pretty tricks," and the stranger, eager to impress him assures him, "I also do miracles!" (82). The old man responds simply that each artist does what he can in his field, and the devil is stupefied: "He began to feel too simple" (83). He is in fact nothing more than a theatrical magician, disappointed at the lack of surprise in his audience even when he does his best trick, returning the filled glass to his hand. It would seem odd that an old man who "liked to wonder at things a lot" (79) is unimpressed by such a display of magic, but he is too busy recalling the past, fantasizing, and observing the marvelous things about him to appreciate the devil's so-called miracles. The other night the sky seemed to show towers of diamonds and he felt childlike wonder toward the stars which seemed to enter his house.

The old man never abandons his courteous demeanor and makes an effort to exhibit some admiration for the stranger's tricks, but prefers the "magic" of the familiar, "Between that glass and the stars there is a big difference, naturally" (83). He is more intrigued by fantasizing about an old cow he had once owned with its mutilated horns replaced by silver and gold ones. How can the devil's cheap bag of tricks compare to the real marvels of nature and to the delights of the imagination? On the other hand, it is not such an easy matter to decide whether the end of the story is miraculous or marvelous. The narrator (who may be Félix Muriel) tells how the old man placed the blank book in the City Hall:

And as long as its folios lasted there were no frauds or embezzlements there. Or even legal suits. And they even made a new road and bought an organ of beautiful tone, since the one they had was out of tune and voiceless." (86).

It could very well be that such progress and the disappearance of these all-too-common public ills represent real miracles!

VII   *"The Rock and the Bird"*

We first meet the protagonist of "La peña y el pájaro" upon his return from travels abroad to his home where he settled family debts, bought his two brothers' shares in the estate, and convinced his aunt to remain in the house with him. But, says the narrator, he

had even then very secret melancholies, avoided perhaps during many years and which he still tried to postpone some time more with the delight and surprise of his return, but which finally opened like a very rare flower, for he is the man in the following story (91).

The man, now approaching fifty years of age, is troubled by his lack of purpose and, searching his memory, recalls a cave beside the sea where a hermit lives. Wandering away from the oak grove where he had been thinking, he encounters a hermit whom he tells about having lost his memory. The hermit says he has no magical powers, only a rock which warns that it is best to scale it or go around in circles. He asks the protagonist, whose name is Anselmo, if he would wish to see his whole past, but the latter sees nothing worth recalling and equates memory with loss of freedom. The compassionate hermit engages in physical struggle with Anselmo, who feels that he is his father and they've fought before. The combat ends in an embrace. The hermit Andrés describes several trials which Anselmo must face, going in circles and alone. Anselmo later sees Andrés retrieve a large stone he had thrown into the pond. He carries it to the cave for him, accepts some nuts, takes leave of his friend, and falls asleep.

Perhaps what follows is a dream, he later confides to a friend. A cart driver named Andrés gives him some nuts, and he finds himself in a wasteland where everything previous seems a dream. He finds one of the nuts empty but a strange odor calls forth memories of his childhood and of his parents. He awakens in the same oak grove he left three days before to seek the hermit. No one can direct him to the place of his meeting with Andrés, but he has three nuts which seem to prove the reality of his adventure. He retains the last nut unopened, refusing his friend's offer to help, saying that no one can open the small nut another has in his head.

Anselmo becomes a taciturn wanderer and leaves the unopened nut with an old man, "the same who had a curious interview with the devil" (106), who promises to open it at an opportune time. Anselmo decides to dispose of his riches, but a poor vinedresser returns his gold, not wishing to contribute to his ruin, and a poor pine cone vendor takes him for Satan buying souls. A group of rowdies come to stalk "the Devil" and beat Anselmo until the sight of his blood makes them realize that he is indeed human.

Anselmo ponders his immense solitude, the value of trying to know himself, and his hunger for all and for nothing. It anguishes him that his words remain while he cannot recall the instant of trial which plunged him into forgetfulness. Returning home amidst the jeers of neighborhood children, he finds that his aunt has declared him incompetent for having given away his estate. He takes nothing seriously, even offering her a proposal to be his widow. She offers her help: "No one is like others think he is. Fight with me, if necessary. That is better than fighting alone, with yourself, or with I don't know what" (119). Anselmo's friend assures him that he shares many of his anxieties, but the forlorn wanderer feels no consolation and calls for charity, a brother, Andrés. "Anselmo," answers a voice from the mountain as Anselmo dies, and the saintly old peasant opens the last nut to find that it is good. The protagonist's search for lost memory and his conversations with his friend suggest that this story is the continuation of the truncated manuscript *Félix Muriel* discarded in "Pliny's Garden" fearing that it would end in nothing.

In this sense it may be considered an invention of Félix Muriel, although he may also be the friend to whom Anselmo confides.

It is always a risky business to try to interpret dreams, and even more so when they are multiple as in this story where we find dreams within other possible dreams and indefinite boundaries between imagination, daydreams, dreams, and "reality." As in a dreamworld, symbolic meaning may be assigned to objects but the symbolism, like that of the title, cannot be entirely explained by logic. Andrés alludes to the rock:

But why insist on seeing through a rock? It would be bad business. We would be left without a rock which, being what it is, impenetrable to sight, realizes its purpose. And if something hides from us that should be seen and the rock itself is not a warning that it isn't good to go further, the proper thing to do is scale it or go around it. If you wish, let us go around (93).

The rock acquires another aspect when the hermit says, "someone has to remain firm when everything else falters. Help me, Anselmo, brother, with your confidence, to keep me firm. Or let's change. You be the rock and I'll be the bird" (99). Anselmo is not content to rest at the rock with Andrés but prefers to wander like a bird, relentlessly searching, yet longing to return to the rock which like his past cannot be recuperated.

The nut seems to suggest the mystery of life and personal reserve, for the only person who can open it, when Anselmo dies, is an old man who we know from a previous story is a saint. Anselmo feels his life has been devoid of meaning; however, the old man who opens the hard nut finds it to be good. This would suggest that Anselmo's life was hard but not without meaning, although he could not perceive it. Perhaps its fullness lay in the search itself. The tenuous light emitted by a firefly in the hermit's cave suggests the luminescence Anselmo pursues, whose light he feels is running out with his own life.

Literary and historical allusions contribute additional perspectives relative to previous human experience. One critic, José María Alfaro, compares the beaten Anselmo to Alonso Quijano, but actually the quixotic nature of Anselmo's plight is much deeper than one episode would indicate, for he may be seen as a Don Quijote whose adventures are dreamlike, intellectual, and philosophical rather than physical.[4] Don Quijote had no problems recognizing himself, however, for he affirms that he is defined by his deeds.

Dieste incorporates several allusions to the *Quijote* which equate his protagonist's hopeless quest with Don Quijote's impossible dream. Like Alonso Quijano, Anselmo is almost fifty and lives at home with a relative and a servant. Anselmo, like Don Quijote, considers penance alone in the mountain, is beaten when he attempts a charitable act, and is object of derision as he returns home from his adventures. The most obvious allusion occurs when Anselmo speaks to his aunt about Oedipus and Sophocles, provoking her response; "I haven't read anything that can cause madness" (119). He may also have invented the blond, green-eyed girl named Elisa who he says gave him some apples and who inspires in him a pure, disinterested love.

Besides all these details, the presentation of information has strong Cervantine overtones when the narrator cites as his sources Anselmo's own writings and the testimony of others, which he says may be false, like that of Cidi Hamete Benengeli in the *Quijote*. He also refers to "the exemplary nature of this story" (108), recalling Cervantes' "exemplary novels." Any allusions suggested by the names of the protagonists should not be construed as mere allegorical representations for, as Andrés indicates, names are simply signs to avoid confusion and "any sign is enough" (94). The name Anselmo, however, does suggest that of Saint Anselm of Canterbury (1033–1109), author of the famous "ontological proof" of God's existence, concluding from the concept we ourselves have of an infinitely perfect being that such a being must necessarily exist. Saint Andrew, one of the first Apostles martyred by crucifixion, suggests a more primitive form of faith which is firm and has no need for rational corroboration. In the hermit Andrés's security and in Anselmo's relentless search there is a contrast similar to that which their respective homonyms represent in Christian thought. We are also reminded of Gracián's *Criticón*, with its contrast between Andrenio representing nature and Critilo culture, in the exploration of the world around them.

In any case, it is not quite clear what Anselmo is searching for because he cannot recall just what it is that he has forgotten! At first it appears that he is seeking self-knowledge using memory as a method, troubled by the ease with which the "ashes of escaping memory" have been blown away by his indifference. His life has no purpose without being defined by his understanding of the past, yet he refuses the hermit's offer of reliving the past because he fears it will imprison and limit him. Anselmo does not want simply to retrieve the past in the same way in which Andrés retrieves the stone from the water, but that is all the hermit can offer him, so he must go on alone. Anselmo feels alienated from a past whose letters form "an inalterable text and even I would not want to alter it, but rather enter it and save it; and if I cannot, ask for help" (115). He has lost the capacity for contemplative memory which could possibly restore meaning to this past.

Another way in which Anselmo tries unsuccessfully to find himself is by deliberately avoiding logical thought, "I let myself talk, I let myself be led, I avoided directing my imagination with intention, I spoke nonsense to the point of not understanding" (113). He also attempts conversation and confession, to no avail, for he ends up calling for Andrés, a brother, but perhaps Andrés is nothing more than his own shadow and his own voice that he yearns to find.

The structure and style of Dieste's story parallel its theme perfectly. The introduction provides a realistic view of the returned wanderer, sure of himself, and in command of his situation, who subsequently becomes an explorer of his own being. The rambling, amorphous structure of the story reflects the uncertain course of the protagonist's struggle in the labyrinth of his forgetfulness. As Gómez Martín notes, the *rodeo* or roundabout technique responds to the hermit's advice that the only way to deal with a rock is to go over it or around in circles.[5] The reader becomes a sort of bird who must go in circles around the story, mysterious and impenetrable like the rock in the title. Like Anselmo's past, the story is written with certain elements of chance, with and without intention. If Anselmo's discussions with the hermit and his friend do not yield understanding, Dieste's invention cannot be expected to do so either. There is deliberate interference with logic and we are confronted by ambiguity and doubt. Communication is not an easy matter. When one can hardly communicate effectively with himself, how can he attempt real communication with others? According to Anselmo, language was the result of joining the individual solitudes of two men speaking to themselves and discovering the possibility of speaking to each other.

There are some really beautiful lyrical passages in the story, as in the metaphorical vision of memory as "ashes that a great wind can sweep away one day, a luminous wind which doesn't respect ashes" (114). This particular quote inspired another Galician writer, the Surrealist E. F. Granell, to write a fanciful short story entitled "El hombre verde" (The Green Man), using Dieste's words as an epigraph upon which he constructs his own fictional mystery.[6] Dieste frequently uses sea images to describe sensations with great lyricism. Anselmo sees rocks "that seemed to have risen like boiling waves" in some remote age (95). The hermit and Anselmo look at each other in a "luminous sea of doubt" and Andrés speaks of sobbing that "attracts like the undertow that pulls at the feet of even the best swimmer" (97). Recalling his childhood, Anselmo describes the sleep of his parents like a "great ship scaring off monsters" and his own as something that "could be gobbled up as stormy high seas devour small boats" (103). The abundance of this marine terminology suggests the protagonist's floundering in a sea of "contrary waves" (114) and his final shipwreck, for at the end he feels on the brink of a world apart like a "drifting ship" (119).

Expressions reminiscent of folklore make Anselmo's adventures seem like an enigmatical fairy tale for adults. This impression is enhanced by the "once upon a time" formula which introduces Anselmo's wanderings, and by expressions such as "they say" and "in some villages, very old people tell . . ." In this way Anselmo becomes part of a popular legend in the mythology Félix Muriel shares with his people.

VIII   *"Charlemagne and Belisarius"*

In the story "Carlomagno y Belisario," beautiful mountain peaks frame the hermitage of San Ramón (Saint Raymond) toward which a group of festive young pilgrims makes its way amid light banter interrupted by an impressive voice, "Brothers, help this creature of God." The people are surprised to see a robust, husky man with the face of "an archaic and serious emperor" (126) and body deformed by tiny childlike arms. The compassionate pilgrims all give him some gift, and animated conversation among the country fellows and girls resumes. A man with a fortune-telling canary, that knows all although "he knows nothing" (127), comes to entertain them, but his piglike features inspire jeers and pointed remarks which he answers calmly. As a child, he says, he cursed his beautiful mother who attributed his looks to her whim for eating pork when she was pregnant, but he told her he exists for some good, to counterbalance the heavenly scales.

In the second part of the story the deformed Charlemagne compliments the ugly Belisarius on his answers to the thoughtless people's comments. The latter responds that the shame of his misfortune drove him out into the world. Charlemagne tells him not to feel ashamed, for lineage takes many turns, with some branches flowered and others frightful; only God can read the loose letters which form a coat of arms. The fortune vendor's "mask" becomes infantile with wonder and then assumes the "remote calm of a forgotten saint" as the other resumes his chant, "Brothers, help this creature of God!"

This story is so masterfully orchestrated that every detail of content and language contributes in some way to the totality. As in previously mentioned stories, Dieste begins with a sort of introduction with description and conversation serving as a prelude to the scene which follows. Two major themes of the story are suggested in the first part, appearance and fate. The crowd, insensitive to the natural beauty around them and "thirsty for marvels," comments about their different jobs as tailors, seamstresses, farmhands, and stoneworkers before seeing Charlemagne, whose tiny arms prevent him from engaging in such manual tasks important to society. The second anonymous dialogue, inspired by Charlemagne's presence, is about "what the eyes see!" (127). In terms that are familiar to them, the pilgrims lament that the seamstress covers what people most want to see and someone again repeats, "What the eyes see!" Another admonishes, "But quiet about this business of seeing, which was mentioned for a more respectful reason." "More respectful, depending. With good or bad fortune, how is one born?" (127).

Charlemagne's deformity inspires the crowd's pity, but Belisarius' ugliness seems a more frightening sight to those attentive only to "what the eyes see." Even their sense of hearing is attuned to the visual, for upon hearing Charlemagne's impressive voice, they pay more attention to what they see; "and with compassion entering through their ears, it sharpened the eyes even more" (126). A *lapsus linguae* or slip of the tongue about the function of the eyes acquires great significance, "Some people close them to pretend to be deaf." "You must mean blind, man." "You understand me; it's the same thing" (127). Unfortunately those who can't see beyond their eyes have equally insensitive ears. "It would be a pleasure to hear him if it weren't for seeing him," says one pilgrim about Belisarius (128). People like beautiful things; for that reason the Charlemagne story which his namesake sometimes sells to earn money "is very beautiful and is in great demand in this land" (129). For the wise

Charlemagne, truth is more important than appearances. He is capable of perceiving much more than the mask that is as distasteful to the pilgrims as to the man condemned to wear it. Belisarius says to the crowd, "I would rather have a mirror before me, with all the horror of seeing myself, than sly whispers" (128).

The important theme of destiny is discussed with regard to Belisarius' fortune-telling canary. "Who can save himself if it is written?" asks a pilgrim. "He who by good fortune or another writing is warned in time," answers Belisarius. He himself, however, feels controlled by destiny which has provided him with a mask that he lets control his actions. He acts out the part his ugly mask has imposed on him by acknowledging that he is a freak, flaunting the ugliness he cannot hide, and inspiring consternation in the girls. Charlemagne, on the other hand, has not allowed himself to be driven by shame or fate but has assumed responsibility for his own destiny in a regal manner befitting his name and emperor's face. He respects Belisarius for his judicious responses to the pilgrims but urges him to feel less ashamed, for by dwelling on his physical grotesqueness, he is making the same mistake as the crowd. He explains to Belisarius that fate is responsible for misfortunes such as theirs and that its designs are inscrutable. Belisarius learns to turn his eyes inward, having found in Charlemagne an attitude which can change what he considered inevitable. As proof of his new "vision" of life, the faded canary now seems prodigious to him, not for its fortune-telling talent but for its inner beauty as "a little miracle of sun and fidelity" in which he sees himself "in a simple mirror of estasy or recognition" (130).

Another theme suggested in the first part of the story is that of perceiving differences and contrasts, as when the pilgrims talk about the seamstress and the tailor who do similar work but are different. Charlemagne and Belisarius are likewise similar in their physical handicaps yet different in their way of dealing with them. The emperor is humble, the general ashamed. There is also a distinction between superstition, represented by the bird, and one's own responsibility for his future. Arturo Serrano Plaja speaks of the presence of charity in Dieste's book, though he apologizes somewhat for suggesting a theme perhaps incompatible with cold literary analysis.[7] It is, however, important in this story for Charlemagne views himself as a human being and, in his chant, "Brothers, help this creature of God," he establishes his brotherhood with others more unfortunate than he as fellow children of

God. He teaches Belisarius the value of charity for self and at the end his call for charity implies that it is not only for himself but also for Belisarius.

The structure of the story also provides a striking contrast between the light repartée of the pilgrims and the elevated conversation of the two protagonists in the second part. Demythification, mentioned previously with reference to other stories, is present only in the sense that physically the characters seem to be sad parodies of their illustrious forebears. Spiritually and intellectually, however, it is more exact to say that there is mythification of the protagonists which elevates them to the dignity of the two heroes their names evoke. The story has an air of remote medieval Galician ambience, particularly notable in the dialogue between Charlemagne and Belisarius, courteous and poetical, archaic in flavor. Charlemagne reiterates his forebear's historical role as guardian of the faith, while the ugly Belisarius carries the name of a Byzantine general (505?–565) who also fought for Christiandom but whose story is less fortunate and long forgotten. When his calm after speaking with Charlemagne is described as that of a "forgotten saint" (130), we are reminded of the original forgotten Belisarius and at the same time of San Ramón, who also seems forgotten by the fun-loving pilgrims who stage a fair at his hermitage, complete with fireworks, tamborines, and bagpipes. Charlemagne retains an inner faith that despite his misfortune enables him to bless others, such as the child (Félix Muriel?) whom he wishes good looks and wisdom, adding, "May you recall this day the rest of your life and remember like a paradise this childhood of such beautiful colors" (126).

IX *"The Insured"*

The story "La asegurada" opens with a mountain girl who questions travellers about their destination or place of departure. A boy tending a cow tells her that he was in the village and takes special care to remind her of the second part of her question which she seems to have forgotten—the red sailboat wasn't there. His mother and a neighbor berate him for offering the information, adding that he knows little of the world. The boy admires the "crazy girl" who is free to roam while he is treated as a child. When he sleeps that night, "all the wisdom of the village enters his soul through the door of dreams" (133); the next day when he awakes, he hopes to see the girl again so he can give her some hope. The next vision of the girl is projected against the magnificent panorama of mountain peaks from which the sea can be observed. We see her delight and wonder at small flowers as she gathers plants, branches, and pebbles to offer to travellers.

Through conversations of the girl's mother, grandfather, and fellow villagers we learn of her uncontrollable wanderings, caused by the prolonged absence of her husband who had left for America a few days after marrying her to insure her faithfulness during the voyage that he had planned previously. The narrator describes the lovers and tells how Eloísa tried, during the first years of separation, to maintain her familiar way of being but felt herself fading into the "elastic time of dreams" (144). The narrator observes Eloísa in the port scrutinizing the boats and watching the ocean, surrounded by playful children, but then he becomes more closely involved. Seeing her on the edge of a cliff with her hands raised toward a gull, he suppresses a cry in order not to frighten her, but now fears having interfered with some heavenly design which he later serves.

Returning from a galleon at night, the narrator sees her running toward him. She embraces him with such emotion that he is momentarily swept up in her love. She bares her breasts playfully and the narrator, fighting against his emotions, refuses to be the object of a love meant for another, though an insidious voice inside berates him for his lack of charity. She seems to realize the mistake, asks if he brings her a message of her husband's death, and insists that this is the day they were meant to come together. Like the moon which disappears and then reappears, Eloísa is gone but he finds her once more. He answers her queries with silence and she leaves while the narrator's heart beats like funeral drums. Shortly thereafter, the news spreads that Eloísa has been found dead at the foot of a cliff. We now realize that the narrator is Félix Muriel when he says that he asked his namesake Don Félix, the doctor, to refrain from disfiguring Eloísa's body by autopsy or her memory by inquiries. He describes her family's grief as they return home.

As in the story of Juana Rial, Félix Muriel comes to feel the depths of close contact with a mysterious being who is as much a creation of the collective imagination as of her particular destiny. In the same way that the reputed witch "bewitches" the villagers as focus of their fantasies, Eloísa also brings a little madness to all who in one way or another touch her life. One section of the narrative is virtually a discussion on madness and the way the people regard it. We learn that "in any respectable region there is always a crazy person and if there aren't any now, there were before," (137). The wild antics of the furious madman make people bless "like a miracle or like a desired dawn this transparent gift of reason" (137), and if he is a quiet madman who thinks he is a king, people (including the narrator) feel they are his subjects and children follow him, proud to be his chamberlains.

The person whom the people have seen go mad becomes an object of respect and mystery:

The people of the country and the shore who depend on the stars and the winds and distinguish youth from old age and know the aroma of the earth disturbed to receive the dead, this old nation is never irreverent with those who go mad; they are not considered merely as inferior beings or broken machines, but as figures that make us shiver or laugh, and they do not isolate them, for they knew them from before, before the enigma of their disturbance, and they are not about to ignore them now because they don't understand them. One must understand them in some way, making a Babel of legends or of farces to grant them some measure of hospitality. And in this fraternal Babel, the whole region becomes a little mad also (137).

In such a fashion everyone, including Félix Muriel, participates in Eloísa's madness. She lends herself to the role which love and destiny have imposed upon her, conscious of her increasing loss of reason, and submits to the frightened respect or compassion of the people realizing that "there is always a madwoman and now I am she." The legend about her is a collective creation formed by her family, the mountain people, and the inhabitants of the port, and this collective fantasy is as vital to her portrait as the narrator's own testimonies and inventions.

Félix Muriel makes us fully conscious of being his audience as he directs his story to us as listeners, but he does not feel the least bit limited by verisimilitude in a conventional sense, for he enjoys complete omniscience which allows him the freedom to use multiple points of view gleaned from hearsay, his own experience, Eloísa's thoughts, and invention to produce an impression of total reality. The narration develops slowly with such digressions as this close-up nautical description of the lovers' faces: "and with reference to their noses, each one saw when they met that they were friends and that they were going to go in the same direction like two ships, though his prow or nose was the leader" (142). This tender description convinces us that it was natural that the lovers both wanted to insure each other's faith in a manner worthy of their great love. This interlude not only brings us into close contact with the lovers, but also gives us a glimpse of the past with an understanding of the great love which the public characterization of Eloísa as the madwoman seems to have forgotten. Later, when we realize the part Félix Muriel played in Eloísa's drama, this digression becomes even more significant as a fantasied scene in which he might have been an actor, at least vicariously. The narrative also includes a story within the story when a harvest hand who had been in Mexico offers his account of difficulties experienced there as possible reasons for Eloísa's husband's prolonged absence.

In "The Insured" Félix Muriel's personal involvement exceeds that of any previous narrative, but we are not aware of his identity until almost the very end. We may surmise that he is also the boy of the first part of the story who volunteers information that the red boat isn't in port, and is berated for his lack of charity. His reply, "That's how people can go mad" (135) points to the alienation and loneliness which he feels now in a very personal way and which subsequently will enable him to sympathize with Eloísa's plight. Later in the story the narrator appears as an observer whose view of reality is influenced by Eloísa's. In this respect he says that her admiration of the boats in the harbor acts as a mirror in which the familiar sights seem unusual. She awakens him by her example to a marvelous world in which the port becomes a riddle and reality may be disguised. He reflects on the possibility that the red boat could be there painted another color, and then finds himself a character in Eloísa's dream, though he has not disguised himself. His emotional meeting with her is the high point of the story, described in nautical images:

And in her whole body a delirium of love so majestic and profound, and with such sudden and gracious crests of tenderness as can only be compared to the sea when it rests and recovers after a storm (149).

Félix accepts the unexpected role of the long-lost Juan for a while, but upon discovering mutual feelings of love, opens Eloísa's eyes to the truth, the truth that kills. The story assumes a circular structure when he repeats the same lack of compassion as the boy in the first scene. He could have contributed to Eloísa's fantasy, which might later be remembered like a dream instead of being the messenger of death. Félix Muriel has reached the ultimate point in his development as a mature human being when he feels responsibility

for Eloísa's death. All he can do afterwards is try to save her body
from mutilation, transform her story into eternal myth, and confess
to us:

Then her death became evident and it seemed that all the rest was far away,
that all had happened a thousand years before or in that remote age that
fades away always, no matter how memory goes back, because it is the
mysterious peak of myths and eternity (156).

From the very first pages the story is filled with irony when a
woman asks Eloísa in Galician: "Why do you come to the Town,
mountain girl? Here there is a lot of confusion. People are crazy"
(148). Early in the story the narrator cites among the causes of
madness "love's misfortunes, which seem like a luxury or something
bearable to someone who has not felt them" (137). Ironically a
similar experience brings him also to the brink of madness when he
says, "I am the crazy one." "Of what importance are disguises?"
(151) he asks and Eloísa seems strangely lucid when she explains
that their appearances have been changed, his by tribulation and
hers by loneliness. The possibility is perfectly logical: Would a
returning Juan be the same who left years before? Is Eloísa the
madwoman the same as the bride he had left?
    The title itself is ironic in that the "insurance" of marriage as
testimony of a great love makes Eloísa sure that Juan will return and
hence ensures her madness. Félix, however, does not have to
accept another's identity and with painful renunciation which he
compares to that of the saints, he is able to extricate himself from
the situation because he is not insured. He first asks the absent Juan
for forgiveness for having kissed Eloísa and appeals to him for
understanding as he excuses his actions:

Eloísa was the purest and most beautiful thing I had had so close.
Afterwards I did what you would have done in my place—changing roles
but leaving love at the same height (150).

Ironically he asks Juan to imagine himself in *his* place when he has
refused to imagine himself in the place of Juan. In any case it is an
impossible love capable of driving anyone mad. Perhaps the
greatest irony of all is the fact that Félix avoids frightening Eloísa by
repressing a cry that may have sent her plunging from the precipice
but later causes her to die in exactly the same way.

The ending of "The Insured" is surprisingly similar to that of
"Juana Rial" in which the young Félix, looking out from the reputed
witch's hut says, "I had seen the sea and the sky and had seen the
gulls and the eyes of an ox" (29) as he feels the huge waves looking at
him and singing. At the end of Eloísa's story he watches the
mourning mother and grandfather ascend the mountain:

> . . . and I follow them, follow them, until the instant of a roar that can
> come from the mountain sky or from the whole village—now in sight—or
> from an immense golden ox in whose eyes my own feel delirium, and which
> I don't know if it calls me or sends me away (156).

In both endings Félix invokes the image of an ox's wide eyes filled
with mystery as an abyss which attracts and repels. Here the golden
ox may be a totemic animal, guardian of the mountain. The image
also suggests the nautical *ojo de buey* or tiny porthole of a ship
through which one observes the world outside, which in both
stories appears strange and hostile from Félix's altered perspective.

X   General Considerations

Although *Félix Muriel* cannot easily be reduced to the designation
of a specific literary genre, it does have an unmistakable unity. The
explicit or implicit presence of Félix is the most obvious unifying
element, but there are others too. For Concha Castroviejo the
constant protagonist is memory, while for Luis Suñén it is the
Galician landscape.[8] Salustiano Martín sees a "halo of magical
fiction" that lends cohesiveness to all the stories.[9] Certainly all these
observations are correct, but since Félix Muriel is the one who
provides the magical vision and the exploration of memory in a
Galician context, his presence, which Gómez Martín has called
"almost phantasmagoric" binds the stories into a unit much like a
novel.[10] There is also a carry over of themes and of some characters
from one story to another.

The question has arisen to what extent Félix Muriel is an alter ego
of Rafael Dieste or a self-portrait, as many critics have suggested. If
we recall Andrés' comment in "The Rock and the Bird" that "any
sign will do" since a name only is useful in its function of facilitating
external recognition, we may assume that Félix may well be
Dieste's alter ego. Although the degree of autobiographical fidelity
is a moot point and has, of course, little to do with the literary value

of the book, the name of the protagonist clearly has autobiographical implications which are of interest to the curious reader. According to information kindly provided by Carmen Dieste, the author's father's name was Eladio Dieste Muriel, following the Spanish custom of using two surnames, the second referring to the mother's name. In addition, the family of Rafael Dieste's paternal grand-mother, María Muriel Rodríguez, included a friar who was also a painter and whose name was precisely Félix Muriel. It may be recalled too that this was the pseudonym the author used in signing some of the articles he wrote for *Nova Galiza* in Barcelona during the Spanish Civil War.

Elisa Dieste Muriel, the author's aunt who never married and who lived with his parents, may be identified perhaps as "Aunt Eulalia" in the story "This Child Is Crazy." Further autobiographical content may be adduced from the story "Pliny's Garden" when the young Félix Muriel throws discarded pages of his manuscript into "Limbo." Carmen has described her husband's custom of writing and then discarding notebooks during the time they were in Paris in 1935. As Dieste worked on his memorandum for the Board of Extension Studies Abroad, he wrote many pages that had nothing to do with his studies of theater or with writing literature but which represented attempts to clarify his own thoughts, which is a major theme in *Félix Muriel*.

The reader of the book is invited to reconstruct an image of Félix Muriel from the various elements provided. In the first two stories he is narrator of his own personal childhood experiences in the setting of his family home. It is evident that he is given to fantasy and possesses an extraordinary sensitivity to that mystery which lies in the familiar. In "The Stuffed Parrot" Félix enlarges the field of his experiences by exploring others' lives as well as his own, absorbing the phantoms of Don Ramón's recall, and feeling the weight of the responsibilities which friendship entails. Félix Muriel is also the narrator of his own inventions such as "The Rock and the Bird," and of other tales which contribute to the folklore of his people as in "The Blank Book," or those which touch him personally, such as "Juana Rial, Flowering Lemon Tree." He may be the boy who is always asking the old man of "The Blank Book" for stories or the one who saddens the insured Eloísa. He grows from a child whose universe is a landing above which a cherry-colored oil lamp emits promises and reflections to a young man considered a friend and advisor by professor Don Julián in "Pliny's Garden", to protagonist

with a difficult role thrust upon him in "The Insured." The doctor in
this story, also named Félix, describes him: "You're a Muriel. You
turned out a little misguided and heretical, but in any case,
upbringing can make up for that" (154).

Félix Muriel continually enriches his experience in unusual ways,
and his marvelous gift for seeing much more than the eye can see is
transmitted to the reader, introducing us to an unknown and
surprising world waiting to be discovered. There are no crystal balls
to recreate magic, but a cherry-colored lamp to provide adventure
and mirrors—which appear in some form in almost all the
stories—to reflect the truth, unexpected views of the familiar, or the
opportunity to observe oneself in the present, something which
otherwise can only be accomplished later by means of memory.

For Dieste memory is the phenomenon of most interest, not that
memory which reproduces data or enables us to discharge errands
and mechanical tasks, but rather contemplative memory which
turns experiences only half-lived or inert into a living memory of
experiences illuminated by creative hindsight. Only memory,
imagination's ability to transcend time, can join the voices of youth
and age of one individual in a simultaneous dialogue ("The Blank
Book") or can reproduce a mother's voice against changing visions of
different moments of life ("The Rock and the Bird"). There is,
however, in Dieste's stories a tension which stems from the
question of whether memory is a blessing or a curse. The ability to
review the past consciously makes man a historical animal capable of
revising his conduct on the basis of what he and others have done
before. It allows him to gain some degree of self-knowledge by
permitting relatively impersonal observation as in a mirror turned
to the past. This is what Anselmo appears to search for in "The Rock
and the Bird," but at the same time he fears the restraints it implies.
In "The Stuffed Parrot," memory is more of a curse, haunting the
present with guilt but also driving Don Ramón to the assuagement
of confession. Don Julián of "Pliny's Garden" feels the weight that
the past imposes in its inexorable nature, recorded by the historian
and never permitted to disappear. The devil's mirror is the dread
book of account in which man's transgressions are remembered for
eternity unless a saintly old man is able to outwit the devil and erase
them by turning his own prodigious memory into a force for charity
("The Blank Book").

Writing itself is a way of achieving a multifaceted view of reality,
allowing reflection upon the past, drawing upon the individual

memory with its adjunct of dreams, fantasies, and doubts, and the collective memory embodied in myths, legends, traditions, and history. In this connection Dieste's repeated use of literary and historical allusion to mythify or demythify brings together individual and collective memory. Reality is in large measure dependent upon one's perception and experience, which leads us to the recurring theme of madness, which in these stories seems to be simply a matter of degree. Félix Muriel's aunt pronounces, "This child is crazy" because she cannot perceive his Orphic metaphysical adventure. There is madness in the collective imagination which sees Juana Rial as a witch and which composes legends to try to understand those who have lost their reason ("The Insured"). In "The Rock and the Bird" and in Eloísa's story, madness is related to the demands of the past which insure or control us and it is always a little contagious. Sometimes reality presents itself in mysterious ways, falsified by the masks of physical appearance or names ("Charlemagne and Belisarius") or imposed quite by chance, as when Félix Muriel is called upon to be an actor in Eloísa's fantasy or when an old man is distracted from his task of shelling beans long enough to redeem his village. It is no wonder that Félix feels guilty, for the business of assuming such awesome roles is a job only saints can handle.

With regard to stylistic elements, the critics have unanimously praised Dieste's prose for its richness, musicality, agility, and delicacy. They do not hesitate to use superlatives to describe it as "one of the most palpitating, effective, and convincing in modern Spanish literature" or to say that "in Rafael Dieste language acquires an expression, a classical tone, a radical beauty not achieved by any other Galician author in the Spanish language since Valle-Inclán." [11] Dieste handles a great variation of tones and styles. He is a master of volume, taking us from noisy scenes of children or festive pilgrims to quiet confidences. In contrast to the silence of omissions and pauses between sections of stories, there are immense roars only heard by Félix Muriel or others attuned to the marvelous. At times encroachments of Galician vocabulary may be detected and structural influences such as the frequent use of progressive forms equivalent to "I am thinking that . . ." (175) or "I am needing" (142), which sound strange in Spanish.

This brings us to consideration of *costumbrista* or regional elements including panoramic views of mountains and the sea. Pilgrimages of country folk and friendly conversations in seaport taverns or village stores provide a close look at life in Galicia without the trappings of conventional regionalism, and finally we touch the heart of Galicia in characters who acquire the stature of folk heroes.

It is likely that Dieste as a writer resembles Félix Muriel, receptive to spontaneous suggestion, chance, and surprise, allowing his stories to develop of their own accord in a Surrealist fashion. As Don Julián asks, "Does a poet always know what he is doing with what he says, no matter how well he knows what he is saying?" (63). Words are orphaned at the moment of utterance; their repercussions may be visible only retrospectively, just like our actions. The road becomes clear after it is travelled, but when it is before us it presents a problem like the rock which may be scaled or circumvented.

These stories respond to an aesthetic concept different from the formula for short fiction offered in *From the Goblin's Archives*, in which the ending is crucial and prefigured in every turn of the story. While Dieste still prepares the subsequent development of his stories by placing significant elements in a first section which acts almost like an introduction, there is less emphasis on unified final effect and longer stories are allowed to meander. His technique of story development is generally one of diffusion here, similar to that described in "Pliny's Garden" as the fragmentary presentation of elements which must be pieced together creatively. By joining together the diverse pieces of Félix Muriel's remembered, imagined, or created experiences, these become indelibly engraved upon our own memory as we emerge from the luminous world of a cherry-colored lamp and an unforgettable book.

CHAPTER 8

Inquiry and Reflection: Essays

DIESTE'S extensive production in diverse fields of knowledge provides ample proof of the tremendous variety of his interests, all of which permeate and inform his imaginative creations of a primarily literary nature. His writings on geometry and philosophy mutually enrich each other and reveal parallel epistemological concerns. In his philosophical *Diálogo de Manuel y David*, for example, he speaks of his attraction to the study of mathematics because of "its mysterious relationship to reality." [1] Our principal consideration of these writings, however, will be based upon a provisional view of the author as a mathematical and philosophical essayist rather than as a mathematician and philosopher, for his original contributions to these fields ultimately must be examined by those who have the expertise to evaluate them competently. Our thrust will be to outline major lines of thought and to point out their relationship to Dieste's overall production in the sphere of the imaginary projection of his ideas or, in other words, to shed light upon his fiction. The divisions of this chapter represent general themes treated in books or in several essays and do not include journalism in the popular press or essays of an occasional nature, some of which are listed in the Primary Bibliography.

I Books on Geometry

Few men of letters are as well versed in mathematics as Rafael Dieste, whose commitment to the discipline, it must be duly noted, is personal and not professional. His dedication to the field for many years has yielded three books which several critics feel might be considered as literature because of their expressive qualities. Domingo García-Sabell, for example, calls *Testamento geométrico* (Geometric Testament) "literary, in the noblest sense of the epithet, in the clarity and elegance of the comparisons, in the excellent order of logical development, in the intimate necessity of the well-used and well-composed metaphor." [2] We would prefer nevertheless to say simply that the prose style has aesthetic qualities. Primarily it serves to achieve effective exposition of ideas and to enhance the content in a fashion that is essentially utilitarian or subservient to that content. We do not feel that literary concerns are at the heart of Dieste's mathematical essays as they are in *Félix Muriel* and they would probably not attract the same type of reader. Despite allegations from a few critics that *Nuevo tratado del Paralelismo* (New Treatise on Parallelism) can be read by the nonspecialist, a competent reading may require more preparation than the average humanist has. The title "Treatise" itself implies a methodical exposition of a specific and even technical problem.

In his *Nuevo Tratado del paralelismo* (New Treatise on Parallelism) Dieste traces the historical vicissitudes of Euclid's fifth postulate, that of parallelism, which through the centuries has either been passively accepted or occasionally questioned by a few alert minds (who became precursors of the non-Euclidean geometries) raising the possibility of whether it could be excluded without undermining the whole Euclidean system. Dieste reopens this problem and, in the words of the Mexican engineer Gabriel Zaid, "on the basis of various hypotheses that in the beginning can be formulated on parallelism, he spreads out a whole order of propositions—to end by showing that it is not possible to exclude the axiom of parallels without contradicting some of the most primary and irreducible premises about figure, space, and movement, the latter understood in its most unequivocal geometric purity." [3]

What may be of greatest interest to the general reader in Dieste's examination of the validity of the fifth postulate is his methodology, carefully explained in the prologue, which in itself is a fascinating essay. He asserts that intuition precedes all recomposition of the unity of an object by logical means which attempt to synthesize it. Intuition is at the base of scientific investigation because it insists on continuing, although reason may repeat that all is formalized and concluded. "It only spreads a marvelous light of agreement, of joyful conformity, when the synthesis presented is at last the mirror itself of the living unity of which it was guardian." [4] The final unity is then "logically illuminated." This amounts to the expansion of scientific methodology and recognition of the power of *a priori* or previous imagination, intuition, and vision, without which logical reason has nothing to apply itself to. This is the inspiration of Dieste's adventure into a question long supposed ended, that of parallelism, which is "that of form in space, and that of the human mind insofar as it anticipates or prepares to 'project' that form" (9).

An interesting stylistic note is the author's use of marine imagery, found extensively in his other writings, to characterize parallelism as "one of the brilliant waves in a sea of questions" (9) and his book as a sea journey whose destination is open, "it is not easy to say the direction of this ship to one who asks from the shore and without previous agreement on the system of signs" (6–7).

¿Qué es un axioma? (What Is an Axiom?), 1967, is a series of essays examining the notion of axiom, a problem originating in the rejection or exclusion in the non-Euclidean geometries of the aforementioned fifth postulate. The author considers such problems as the relationship between the concepts of time and velocity which permit time to be perceived by temporal measure, the geometrical finite nature of the physical universe, the infinity of space, and the role of intuition in yielding an axiom which "is only a sign, a little light of authentic freedom, a promise . . . of mutual understanding not yet agreed upon, of free intersubjectivity" (55).[5] Extending the attitude proposed in *New Treatise on Parallelism*, he describes preaxiomatic investigation inspired by intuition,

to look for a rule is to suspect or guess that it exists. And to consider it good, to render it that confidence is to recognize at once its existence, to say with surprise: Here is the rule: certain and mysterious (85).

The axiom, then, becomes a sign worthy of confidence, a convention. Dieste links this to poetry in that prophecy or foresight precedes *poiesis* (creation, production) with the poet (*vate*, in Spanish) serving as a diviner or *vate*cinator. "Mobility and Similarity," the final thesis explored in the book, confirms the interdependence of the postulate of similarity (equivalent to that of Euclid) and the principle of free movement.

The third and most recent work, *Testamento geométrico* (Geometric Testament), 1975, consists of three "books." The first, "Introduction to Euclid, Lobatschevski, and Riemann," offers a synopsis of the "three geometries"; the second, "Movements in Geometry," justifies the use of the notion of movement; the final book, "Three Demonstrations of the V Postulate," proves the incompatibility of the notion of movement with the exclusion of Euclid's postulate. A number of fascinating implications of these mathematical speculations can be detected in Dieste's fiction in which they are sometimes projected imaginatively. Time and movement, for example, are inextricably linked together in protagonists who not only move about in space, that is from one point to another, but also in time by means of memory or reenacted experience. Even Dieste's verse may be characterized as poetry in movement, filled with dramatic mobility, constant kinesis, not limited to place-to-place movement but representing dramatism and change.

Domingo García-Sabell's introductory essay, "Illuminated Intuition," alludes to Dieste's desire to go beyond verbal or symbolical convenants to the concrete reality of our world. This same desire is evident in many of his characters in search of authentic reality in others and in the self, for whom words, names, and signs are arbitrary and provisional, not always understood when there is no established agreement. Dieste says of all three books of *Geometric Testament* that they are designed to produce an "active, responsible, and dramatic comprehension" on the part of the reader in the spirit of a dialogue (15). His theater is also an open-ended dialogue which no amount of analysis can exhaust or consider resolved. In his preliminary note to *Geometric Testament* Dieste suggests that the "abyssal backgrounds" of the concept of space "may only show themselves dioptrically, through the glass of hypotheses" (15). Perhaps literature itself can be considered a dioptric representation of other unfathomable questions about life and the world. The repeated presence of mirrors, reenactments, and memories in Dieste's fiction are means of reflecting reality or truth in the same way that in mathematics the "glass of hypotheses" seeks to show it.

The author justifies his multifaceted approach in *Geometric Testament*, which presents three demonstrations of Postulate V when he might have chosen any one:

But it isn't superfluous when the purpose is not only to "demonstrate," but also to investigate, to show that what is treated is presented in different lights or in various perspectives (16).

To cite just one counterpart in Dieste's fiction, Don Frontán's wrongdoing is confirmed in a number of ways—reflected in his own feelings of guilt, alluded to by other characters, and reenacted in a playlet. While this is not to say that Dieste applies geometrical methodology directly to his literary creations, it does suggest that his view of life is consistent in literature and in science with the intuitive perception of mystery which remains to be discovered and examined in multiple facets.

II   Philosophical Writings

Luchas con el desconfiado (Struggles with the Distrustful) was published in Buenos Aires in 1948 and is presently under revision. This tendency to reorganize, revise, and change somewhat his previously published works corresponds to similar practices with his early fiction in Galician and selected plays and reveals a certain faithfulness to a personal unity and vision. It is significant that Dieste does not refute or make profound changes but rather returns to the original work and adjusts it to new insights.

The preliminary note describes the author's surprise before the work created and in discovering the dramatic complicity existing between the two major parts which compose it. This attitude anticipates the ideas developed in the essays themselves, with the importance Dieste accords to both prevision and postvision in yielding knowledge and to what he calls "contemplative freedom." Reducing the carefully developed chapters of the first part of the book to a provisional synthesis would be no more effective in recreating for the reader the philosophical thought processes contained in them than a skeleton is in portraying a particular individual. By changing the word Platonic to Diestean, we can justify, with the author's own statement, our not providing such a comprehensive summary: "Naturally Platonic thought cannot be summarized. Not only because of its very powerful vitality, but because it was a process of illumination, growing and consequential . . . that still continues." [6]

The basic question which Dieste examines is that of the "ingenuous empiricist" who asks if things are the cause of our knowledge of them. The author only concedes that the concrete reality of objects precedes our experience with them and provides material which is a potential source of knowledge but does not predetermine it. Experience with things is the beginning of cognition, yielding notions but, unless accompanied by what Dieste calls "a determined interest," may be merely comparable to looking at something without really seeing it. Discerning perception primarily occurs in the area of a previous contemplative indetermination designated as "the foyer of judgment" which opens experience to infinite contemplative possibilities. If objects were causes of empirical knowledge, judgment would be reactive, fixed and the same, and therefore not free. The notions yielded by experience, then, are a seedbed of latent future judgments, memories, and even fantasies.

One chapter entitled "Contemplation of a Memory" provides a graphic example of the creative (or re-creative) process in the combination of a child's awareness and receptivity with the reflective and contemplative powers of an adult, which may be seen in *Félix Muriel*. The prose is tinged with lyricism:

Here is a blue pastry pan. (A considerable number of years ago . . .) It is in the window at street level. One who passes by some days and stops unintentionally to see that blue, to submerge himself in it, in its nocturnal depth through which he sees that of day enter within to return as if transfigured and aware and with some secret that it could say, is a child, a child dazed at times—as at that moment—and who, if I remember well, was I myself (69).

The child's indelible notion was of "blue that exists" without constituting a clear and conscious judgment. Now, in retrospect, the author can describe what the awed child could not, and from that remembered sensation of the intense blue object emerge names and people from its "distant closeness." The reader will recognize in this contemplative experience the same sort of mnemonic reflection which permits the lyrical recreation of the past in *Félix Muriel*, where a cherry-colored lamp evokes a whole world of childhood, and a dark parlor provides a voyage to the netherworld. Surely at the time the child could not express the meaning inherent in the experiences which years later are revived, restored, and appreciated by means of free contemplation.

The chapter entitled "Space and Time as Real Conditions of Perception and of the Ostensible World" treats the interdependence of time and space, a subject which appears also in Dieste's essays on geometry. A point can be successively in two different places but not in both at the same time or it would be two points, he explains. This leads to a discussion of the human ability to temporalize as simultaneous or coexisting that which in fact occurs successively, making possible communication and permitting synthesis and judgment, which respond to an aesthetic need to perceive unity. Contemplation in time and with one's own individuation in space permits us to recognize ourselves as sensible beings, to distinguish what is intimate from that which is not and to form notions of the world and the ostensible world. All this comes into play in the interiorization of the ostensible world which is evident in the poetry of *Loving Red Lantern* and in *Félix Muriel*. As we have noted, the experiences and tales recounted are all filtered through the sensitive consciousness of Félix Muriel, whether he be present or absent in the stories, and it is this individuation which provides a sensation of unity to what otherwise might seem unrelated perceptions.

The second part of the book, entitled "The Soul and the Mirror," is essentially introspective discussion with the added literary touch of epistolary form involving the author, a hypothetical friend of his given the name of Esteban by a reader, and the latter, who assumes the role of his apologist and also writes letters. The essay opens with the author's contemplation of a young man's experience (his own, perhaps) in reading Dostoievsky and feeling "alluded to," a process which allows one to gain self-knowledge by reading. He invites the reader to feel alluded to as he describes his correspondence with a young friend who is disillusioned by the insincerity he finds around him and yearns for something in which to believe. The author's attempt to console his young friend and his recommendations of positive reflection upon readings of Dostoievsky and Nietzsche are criticized by the "meditations and sarcasms of Esteban's apologist," a supposed reader who defends the young man's distrust in everything in view of the fact that even man's attempts to know himself involve inevitable insincerity and hypocrisy. According to the apologist,

the principle of identity fails in dealing with man. *A* is *A* but I am not I. If I were the same as myself there would be no reason to advise me to seek the identification of my authentic being (186).

He describes his lack of authenticity and the radical falseness of his being:

I am not in my power, I have never been, I do not know my reason for being, I encounter myself as I would a stranger, and I say in addition that I cannot repeat myself, remake myself, as I repeat a circle (186). . . . I am double because I distrust myself, because I do not know myself, because I am for me an unfathomable being and one who also wants and does not want to be unfathomable (187).

I distrust myself as a witness and nevertheless I have to trust this doubtful witness in order to know who I am (204).

For Esteban's apologist man possesses marvelous faculties which he does not fully control:

> Something is clear for me, that I am unknown—I use reason and senses and what I call memory, understanding and volition—of an unknown being . . . To feel, think, recall, desire, speak are strange, very strange operations which nevertheless I call mine (189–90).

Yet we hypocritically give the impression of having a comprehensible identity by means of "masks," the name and appearance by which we are recognized. If we struggle to understand ourselves, it is because we have not been sincere, even to ourselves, but the desire for self-knowledge is conflicting, for we are anxious to banish enigmas but at the same time fearful of doing so because it would be limiting ourselves, becoming as familiar and predictable as a circle which can be repeated identically again and again. The "struggle" of Dieste's title is with the self, and it becomes clear that all the characters who take part in the epistolary dialogue represent in one form or another the author himself airing different points of view on the problem of self-knowledge.

The essay closes with a consideration of "introspective light and dramatic reflection," and characterizes literary creation as an effort to represent man with grace and dignity "as a patent sign of his own transcendency," and to help him to understand himself without annihilating himself. But Dieste also views literary creation from the reader's point of view when he can discover others' impulses as his own by reflection. The height of feeling so evoked makes one's soul a "dramatic universe," from which the ceremonial and sacred nature of ancient tragedy and the profound responsibility of all poetry is derived. Before the awe educed by human expression, Dieste says, "we know not what we say! Praised be speech!" (216).

"The Soul and the Mirror" is a key essay for interpreting Dieste's fiction in which the theme of self-understanding is a persistent concern elaborated in multiple artistic forms. The author's advice to his friend that he try to contemplate himself from the opposite sidewalk or, in other words, at a distance, is illustrated by Don Frontán's desire to see his own conduct from a different perspective by contemplating it in the form of a puppet show. Doña Luparia who, as the reader will recall, expresses surprise at her own words, discovers in herself another dimension as she contemplates her image in the mirror held by the lovers she has unwittingly brought

together. In "The Rock and the Bird," Anselmo seeks the hermit
Andrés in his frantic attempt to know himself and understand his
past, but at the same time he fears success, "I don't want to limit
myself by knowing myself." [7] Anselmo appears to be afflicted with
the same anxieties as expressed by Esteban, but they are also
present in other characters in the author's fiction, who marvel at
themselves and their words, who do not understand themselves, or
who try to do so not without fear before the terror that self-
knowledge may entail. Masks, names, and signs in Dieste's plays
and stories may be seen as arbitrary instruments of our hypocrisy by
means of which we try to convince others and ourselves that we
know who we are. Don Frontán in fact anticipates words of this
essay when he speaks of labyrinths, closed doors, and how bad a
witness man is of himself.

"The Soul and the Mirror" provides valuable insights into
theoretical aspects of our author's philosophical concerns reflected
in his poetry, drama, and stories, but at the same time it should be
noted that the essay itself exhibits literary concerns. It employs
dialogue, letters, and the invention of characters and is both
expository and entertaining. Esteban at one point even chides the
author for his confusing syllogisms and Dieste teases the reader (and
himself) with serious playfulness when the apologist writes, "I am
speaking of myself but suppose you will feel alluded to" (188) or
says, "Don't believe me more than up to a certain point" (192). The
author also warns that his apocryphal series of letters could possibly
be true. In fact the young reader of Dostoievski, the author who
appears in the essay, his friend Esteban, and the reader apologist
may all be considered as "truthful fictions." The invention of alter
egos to engage in dialogue provides mirrors for the author enabling
him to achieve the multiple views visible only when we try to
observe ourselves (as he advises Esteban) from the opposite
sidewalk or speak to ourselves with the dramatic spirit of the
Unamunian "autodialogue."

A similar procedure is used in *Diálogo de Manuel y David*
(Dialogue of Manuel and David), 1965, which Dieste calls an
"exercise in dramatic reflection" rather than a philosophical
dialogue since Manuel does not strive to overcome David dialectically but rather to engage him in cordial and spirited dialogue which
the reader is invited to continue. Manuel is a modern follower of his
namesake Immanuel (Manuel in Spanish) Kant, the eighteenth-
century German philosopher who in his *Critique of Pure Reason*

examines the bases of human knowledge, recognizing the validity of
a priori propositions not based on sense perception, as well as that of
empirical knowledge depending entirely on such perception.
David, true to his philosopher namesake David Hume, believes
that reason and rational judgment are merely habitual associations
of distinct sensations or experience. Hume, a Scottish thinker and
contemporary of Kant, wrote an abstruse *Treatise on Human Nature*
and *Inquiry Concerning Human Understanding*, but later expressed himself in light essay form or in dialogues, much in the way
that Dieste prefers to do.

The author explains in his introduction that Manuel is responsible
for David's presence. Citing the examples of Cervantes, Pirandello,
and Unamuno, well-known creators of autonomous protagonists,
Dieste places his modern philosophers in a novelesque situation
with David's having been cordially summoned from his ship by
Manuel. The dialogue itself is viewed as a sort of trip or journey
which Manuel has proposed to clarify his thoughts, confident of
their ultimate agreement, "Luckily you are here to understand me
or to make me understand myself" (22).[8] Manuel maintains that
Hume did not pay enough attention to the the question of Habit,
what Kant called forms or laws, and asks David, "Can Habit inspire
the belief in the harmony and regularity of the world—which
amounts to giving birth in our minds to the notion of world, perhaps
to the world itself?" (16). For Manuel, Hume did not distinguish
between expectation and repetition.

David affirms that all belief is a posteriori, or in other words, that
seeing is believing. The rule is arrived at from repeated experience.
Manuel, on the other hand, blames a posteriori reasoning for many
problems of today's world and defends belief a priori—believing is
seeing, for if habits seem to determine beliefs, it is only because
there is some subjective predisposition to acquire habits that
determine beliefs, which are impossible without prior faith.
According to Manuel we must believe first in order to see or, as
David interprets it, *admirar antes de mirar* (in approximate
translation, to foresee before seeing). Manuel insists that there is no
understanding "without imagination and without the lights of
anticipated love" (60). Manuel has the impression that David is
drawing closer to his way of thinking and, as they take leave
fraternally, he tells him how even the habitual lighting of a match
scares him a little: "It is a small example that makes me see in the
manifest fire that which is hidden, and this not only in its ability to

burn, but also in some way, in my possible operations, known and unknown" (69). He never forgets the primary source of wonder that recreates itself in repeated "miracles"; much in the same way that Félix Muriel sees "great familiarity and vast mystery" in the things about him, the poet Dieste finds ample reasons for wonder even in a simple red lantern, and the Guest in *Perdition* encounters novelty in the sun which dawns each day.

As David returns to his ship, Manuel realizes that David is not as convinced as he thought. Perhaps the two ways of looking at Habit are irreconcilable, Habit as foresight confirmed by repetition (Manuel) or as hindsight arrived at by repetition (David). Hume's disciple simply calls previous things causes and others effects. Manuel maintains that somewhere in repetition there must exist a "first moment of believing" (71) which then makes repetition significant in proving the validity of that foresight, for how else could we grasp, invent, or desire what we haven't seen?

The difference between the two views has implications with regard to an orientation to life, for Manuel is apt to view the world with a primeval sense of wonder and discovery (like Dieste, Félix Muriel, and the old man in "The Blank Book"), while David simply accepts what has been "proven" by repetition. Dieste's obvious preference for Manuel is in perfect accord with his attitudes toward geometrical knowledge expressed in *What Is an Axiom?*, where he describes the role of intuition in promoting and orienting the deductive process. An axiom may be considered the mathematical counterpart of habit in that it is a codified habit or rule. Finally, it is evident that for Dieste philosophy is cordial and fraternal dialogue without tenets or dogma. He recognizes the difficulty of convincing others or oneself for that matter, especially when divergent views sometimes appear to overlap. His imaginative projection of the problem of habit is both effective and aesthetically pleasing. As Andrés Torres Queiruga comments, "The ideas are translated and transparent in symbols; logical play is at the same time poetic play." [9]

The other two essays included in *Dialogue of Manuel and David* are somewhat more technical. "La paloma equis" (Dove X) treats the notion of World and Perceptible World *(Mundo Sensible)* using the lyrical symbol of the dove as a paradigm or model dialectically replaceable by any other sensitive beings it may evoke for us. Dieste concludes that one's individual and personalized world (that of Félix Muriel, for example) is not really separable from the World itself and is not possible without it.

The final division of the book contains three "Variations on Zeno of Elea," a fifth-century B.C. Greek mathematician and philosopher who sought to discredit the validity of appearance and sense perception by means of complex intellectual puzzles. Dieste reproduces two famous mathematical fables by which Zeno shows the logical impossibility of motion. In the first Achilles in a race with a turtle cannot arrive at his goal because he has to reach the point ahead which his rival has already left, having had a head start, before he can go on to the next point the turtle has reached, and since the turtle has always left that point earlier he will always be at a point ahead of Achilles. In the other a runner cannot reach a goal because he must continually traverse half the distance, then half the remaining distance, ad infinitum. In effect Zeno negates all progressions by expanding them to prove that a spatial distance cannot be covered in finite time and since movement involves traversing the distance between two points, it does not exist.

This three-part essay shows Dieste's preference for philosophical discussion by means of a variation of methods, in this case a "traditional perspective of Zeno's arguments," followed by a dialogue between Zeno and a friend, and finally a recapitulation in which the author prolongs the consequences of the dialogue in a soliloquy matching wits with Zeno, whose logic is self defeating. "Infinity, Space, Time, Logos, Being, Appearance . . . Who could—or *would*—cage these birds? Let the enormous shadow of other wings move anew our reverence and, incessantly, our sails" (157), concludes Dieste. He detects in Zeno the fear of being right, for no one would be the winner if all the mysteries of life and our world could be resolved dialectically.

III   On Tragedy and History

Any attempt to classify Dieste's book *La vieja piel del mundo* (The Old Skin of the World), 1936, would have to be arbitrary and provisional, for while its subtitle states that it is "about the origin of tragedy and the figure of history," it approaches philosophy and even poetry because of its lyrical prose and abundant use of symbol, metaphor, and myth. The twenty-two short chapters bear a great resemblance to *Loving Red Lantern*, which belongs to roughly the same period of the author's works. There is a similar tendency toward baroque expression and it contains some of the same philosophical themes as his poetry. It is a rather demanding work to read, with the metaphorical flow of the author's intuitions loosely structured following the open course of his reflections on the ideas of Universe and Destiny.

The title and subtitle suggest the age-old dramatic problem of man's individual destiny posed against universal history which both sustains and involves him. The theme is developed in terms of classical myths in line with Dieste's statement:

And it will be seen that there is neither play nor paradox in all this when at last the deep and auroral seriousness of myths is understood, for they are not allegory or dream in which the image anticipates the concept, but zodiacal memory in which the existence of a historical universe is expressed or named. [10]

In Dieste's mythification of history, Apollo with his perfect lyre represents harmony, mathematics, and the principle of individuation, while Mercury with his incomplete, rudimentary lyre made from a slow turtle's shell gives rise to metaphysics with its impatience and anguish, and to the desire to reason. Mercury, the messenger who goes from one point to another, eventually tires of the same pendulum swing from cause to effect and vice versa and brings his heart to be recast at Vulcan's forge. Dionysus is the force of passion, love of life, promise, creation, and youth and is therefore father of tragedy. Dieste describes in impressionist and lyrical prose the birth of tragedy in the gathering of grapes or festivals in honor of Dionysus, when stories of those absent or dead were enacted. Thus the "dance of memory" became "messenger between metaphysical and existential space" (47) which recalls the past but also moves forward, promising eternal youth. And so Dionysus was transformed, becoming more grave and discovering time, memory, and history.

In the mythological discussion we pass through various time frames—Genesis, ancient Greece, the dawn of Christianity, and Socrates, Plato, Leibnitz, Voltaire, Goethe, Rousseau, Kant, and Nietzsche appear in the mysterious light of great myths and at the same time in very human terms. Dieste does not object to the ideas of Nietzsche's early book *The Origin of Tragedy* but does oppose assimilating the Dionysian principle in the concept of Will defined by Schopenhauer in *The World as Will and Representation*. For Dieste the concurrent principles which Nietzsche calls Dionysian and Apollonian do not in themselves constitute tragedy although they are present in its predecessors the dithyramb and certain ritual dances. They are joined by another principle represented by the swift and communicative Mercury (Hermes), Apollo's friend who contributes the relation of means to end, making possible dramatic action and dialogue, which for the Greeks included that of man with the gods. These initial principles, seen as modes of understanding the "historical universe," are extended to include the contemplation of figures and events not strictly mythological but linked to myth metaphorically.

In his story (or myth) "Doblez del signo" (Duality of the Sign), Dieste speaks of the sign as "a double mirror that seemed to be one" and of man's dual nature, which appears in his fiction and poetry often associated with mirrors. This essay also provides some clarification of the father image in these works as representing the light of origin, complete love, and integral memory, while the feminine image evokes repose and forgetfulness. Although he does not develop fully here the open dialogue technique found in his later philosophical essays, it is anticipated in indirect dialogue and the play of thesis and antithesis (as in the "Novela de los dos desnovelados," Novel of the Two Unnoveled People) which Dieste views in retrospect as an expression of the conflicting conscience of youth before the Spanish Civil War.[11]

The book concludes with the vision of tragedy resting on the opposition between universal history and personal destiny:

> In the desire to find sense in time lies the true origin of tragedy. The duality of principles upon which it rests is unequivocal. It is not the opposition between fatality and will, or between an impulsive flash and the principle of individuation, but rather between universal history and personal destiny. Our lives, with those of the immortals, compose universal history—that which is seen and that which is hidden. But our history—that which we believe to be our history—is not, perhaps, universal. And it is tragic to be chosen by a prophecy, by a warning of universal history that we must sacrifice our history. What love or what frightening destiny chooses us? The Greek assembly was witness to that mystery, to that double principle that is in the face of the chosen (158).

Dieste continues to examine the same question several years later in "Pliny's Garden," in discussions between the history professor

Don Julián and his young student friend Félix Muriel referring to
the multitudinous impersonal etceteras of history from which it is
difficult to salvage personal history. Perhaps the author was
reflecting upon how his own personal destiny was affected by the
Civil War. Don Julián and Félix Muriel find that individual history
can be "saved" to some extent by exercising "live memory" in
contrast to the "inert memory" of textbook history and by making
decisions on the personal level.

Ironically *The Old Skin of the World* was published just before
the outbreak of the Spanish Civil War, an event that wreaked havoc
with many personal destinies. Although the book could not receive
usual coverage in journals that would have been possible in normal
times, Manuel Altolaguirre, writing in the first issue of *Hora de
Espana* in January 1937, found it especially significant in that
moment of war when poets were again called upon to celebrate the
deeds of their heroes as in the dawn of theater at the festivals in
honor of Dionysus.

IV   *Reflections on Language*

Dieste's speech in Galician "A vontade de estilo na fala popular"
(Stylistic Motivation in Popular Speech), read upon his reception
into the Royal Galician Academy on April 18, 1970, shows yet
another aspect of his intellectual endeavors. He treats the problem
of normative grammar versus popular usage which he views as a
seedbed for new forms which may vitalize language or corrupt it.
The liberal grammarian thus sees the need for codification and
exposition of some normative system to give live language "a mirror
in which to compose itself." Dieste, however, interiorizes the
problem, considering prescribing norms as inherent in language
itself, as an intralinguistic force. He traces the origins of normative
grammar to the early popular bards who depended on formalities of
rhythm, symmetry, and contrasts naturally imposed by the need for
recall, so that these poets were informal counselors and gramma-
rians. Dieste recognizes that Galician, coexisting with Castilian
which has at its disposal greater means of dissemination, requires
special care to sustain and at times restore its purity without
implying inflexibility.

The common people, he maintains, are perfectly aware of *galego
verdá* (true Galician) and of syntactic, phonetic, and lexical devia-

tions which may arise from misguided concepts of style, affectation, refinement, or prestige. He is optimistic that popular acceptance of deviations is both selective and temporary, so that normative grammar in its function of practical orientation should take into account the popular aesthetic sense which serves as stylistic motivation. These views have implications for the interpretation and appreciation of the author's inventive literature, particularly in the vernacular. His interest in revising and refining his early works in Galician attests to his pride in the language as the expression of an idiomatic community. His faith in the common people—who are the protagonists of his fiction—is evidenced in the essay. His examples of individuals who use artificial modes of speech for prestige remind us of Don Miguel of *The Empty Window* who allows himself to be convinced by his wife and daughter to accept something which is incompatible with his real nature and experience as a Galician sailor. With proper guidance, however, in this case collective pressure, his inner integrity wins out. Thus the community's interests, be they spiritual or linguistic, are preserved and what is authentically Galician or *enxebre* is protected, not by external authoritarian impositions, but rather by community consciousness exerting itself in a natural fashion.

The essay contains some very graphic anecdotes and metaphorical parallels such as his description of grammatical relationships in familial terms or his relating usage to grammar as temperature to a thermometer which obviously has no right to impose its limits on the temperature it registers. His reflections are inhanced by vivid narrative expression, which is that of a good storyteller.

A similar attitude of reasonable and flexible observance toward prescribing norms is recommended in Dieste's *Pequeña clave ortográfica* (Small Orthographic Key) published years earlier, in 1956. Within the pedagogical intent, the prose in this clear, helpful manual of spelling and punctuation is pleasantly conversational, almost hinting at dialogue and anticipating questions a reader might ask. Observations and interesting literary examples accompany the rules. Dieste's approach is broad, accents are related to such considerations as melody and intonation and the rules of punctuation take into account functions of syntax, expression, and even emotion. The author puts normative grammar into perspective, "rules orient us if first we have interpreted them well with alert attention and true rigor." [12]

V *On Painting and Painters*

One of the author's deep and abiding interests is painting. Before
the Civil War, he lectured extensively on art in general or on
Galician painters in various cultural centers of Galicia. Later, in
Montevideo, Buenos Aires, and Monterrey (Mexico) he offered
several lecture series in universities and other centers on Galician
artists, specific art themes, and on Goya, Velázquez, El Greco, and
Kandinski. After his return to Spain, Dieste participated in art
seminars and lectures of the Laboratorio de Formas de Galicia and
the Sargadelos Gallery in Madrid. Painting is also present in
Dieste's writings, in the controversial portrait in his play *The Empty
Window* and in the use of beautiful and sensitive sketches by the
Galician artist Luis Seoane as illustrations in *From the Goblin's
Archives* and the Argentine edition of *Félix Muriel*. A line drawing
of Dionysus by Ramón Gaya appears in *The Old Skin of the World*
and two vignettes by Seoane and a portrait of Dieste by Colmeiro
grace the pages of *Loving Red Lantern*.

In an essay first entitled "Pintura ensimismada y fuera de sí"
(Painting Looking Within Itself and Without) and later "Expre-
siónismo" (Expressionism), Dieste examines the pictorial tenden-
cies beginning with Impressionism which liberated painting from
fidelity to an exterior model, allowing different forms of subjectiv-
ity, with increasing displacement of the center of attention from the
outside object to the poet's personal intimacy. This culminated in
Expressionism, which expresses the object so that it is really an
expression of the artist himself. Noting a "conflict of conscience" in
art, the author advises not a return to the object but rather to the
world, accompanied by an attitude of reverence.

One of the principal themes developed in *Colmeiro: Brief
Discourse About Painting with the Example of a Painter*, 1941, and
discussed previously with relation to *The Empty Window*, is that of
aesthetic unity, which in Colmeiro is "the virtue of integrity" (6),
something much more profound than what is commonly understood
as composition.[13] In Colmeiro agreement and articulation of form,
density, volume, light, line, structure, and color are not obtained by
proportional representation of each but by the artist's accenting
particular elements determined by "truthful grace" rather than by
equilibrium. In the catalogue accompanying the exhibit of works of
Luis Seoane in the Aele Gallery in Madrid on May 28, 1975, Dieste
again stresses the harmony of the whole rather than individual

elements. This importance which he accords to the unity of a work of art is comparable to its conception in a mathematical context with intuition as promoter of the deductive process which may permit unity to be logically illuminated. It would seem that aesthetic pleasure likewise stems from an intuitive perception of an integral unity which the creative artist freely achieves by his intuition rather than by a studied attempt to divide art into convenient categories for analysis.

Dieste's contribution to the catalogue of Laxeiro's exhibit in the Velázquez Gallery in Buenos Aires in August 1958 provides a particularly fascinating example of critical creativity, presenting a series of twenty short aphorisms, highly imaginative improvisations stimulated by the paintings. Three examples concerning masks, dreams, and imagination, and the complex nature of reality may be reflected upon with relation to Dieste's writings:

11 Dreams sometimes go about in search of a dreamer and make strange insinuations—in the cracks of a wall, in the gestures of a rag, in the trembling of a hawthorne—so that we will dream them.

12 A toad can have escaped from a jeweler's hands, be a devil imprisoned (imprisoned in the skin of a toad), or a great bewitched king, and, strangely enough, it can also be simply a toad. How should a toad—or a jewel, or a demon, or a great king—be painted if one does not know these things? Ah, how little is taught in the academies.

In Dieste's 1975 essay and lecture "La estética pictórica de Carlos Maside (con alusiones a otros pintores gallegos coetáneos)" (The Pictorial Aesthetics of Carlos Maside with Allusions to Other Contemporary Galician Painters), he examines this artist's aesthetic ideas as derived or deduced from the pictures themselves, and much of what he says about Maside reveals a good deal about his own preferences. He admires Maside's ability to confer singularity upon the subject as a person, "above all like a friend, but also like a person with his mystery." [14] He contrasts this to Castelao's "extraordinary power of typification." For Dieste, Maside succeeds in discovering the transcendence and mystery of the singular in its setting, revealing its eternity rather than evanescence in the impressionistic manner. He denies the supposed diffusive pantheism attributed to Galicians, recognizing instead

a particular ontological conscience . . . a sort of ontological fury, a desire for things to really exist, a desire that they last, not for their exterior hardness, for the mask that can be placed on them, be it material or formal, but rather deeply felt, interior, so that the durability manifested in an exterior manner is no more than the sign, the light, the message of something profoundly solid—solid like the being—which is found within and forms what later appears with that aspect of exterior permanence (94).

He finds in Galician artists: Souto, Seoane, Laxeiro, Maruja Mallo, Colmeiro, and Maside a common ability to attain *transpintura* ("transpainting") which reveals what is behind the masks of exterior display.

It would seem that Dieste shares this Galician tendency described in the essay, for his own writings seek to become transliterature, to penetrate masks, signs, and words and go beyond the outside view of things by means of interiorization and the exploration of memory. The mystery in humble things which he ascribes to Maside also characterizes his own creations, as well as the spirit of friendship (which he finds in Seoane) and cordiality. Like Maside, Dieste has not made a precise statement of his aesthetics, but they are implicit in his works. The essay on Maside is especially valuable in giving the reader an idea of what Dieste thinks about criticism, at least with regard to painting. He speaks of some books on art which spoil the delight of contemplation with their explanations which take the fun out of interpretation and make the mystery disappear. The author would prefer to adopt an attitude of respect before the mysteries which ideally promote the observer's own creative responses. His concept of criticism seems to eschew precepts and arbitrary categories in favor of the free exercise of intellectual and imaginative analysis derived from the work itself and the critic's intuition.

CHAPTER 9
Summary and Conclusions

R AFAEL Dieste's writings span over fifty years of creative work
and include every genre; yet within this diversity of form and
subject there is an organic consistency shown in his tendency to
return to previously published works and revise them. It is as if they
were a nucleus, like that of a man's own unique and identifiable
nature, from which growth and changes originate in the process we
call life, always open and responsive to the unexpected and
unforseeable. Dieste is a reader as well as an author, and returning
to his earlier works he finds possibilities for new growth enriched by
new insights at the same time that he undertakes new and varied
projects.

Perhaps the most distinguishing characteristic of the author's
fiction is his philosophical motivation, documented in his discursive
works and transformed into poetry in the broadest sense of the word
in his imaginative works. Both his philosophical inquiry and his
literary expression respond to ontological and epistemological
concerns which are too vital to be entrusted only to reason. Dieste
has great faith in intuition, inspiration, and imagination, and it is
from these roots that his inventive muse springs. His defense of free
reflection is not simply a theoretical attitude; it is evidenced in the
unrestricted freedom he allows his characters in following their own
courses unhindered by a destiny imposed by the author. They are
marked by an essential dignity, be they vagabonds, sailors,
pilgrims, plain folk, or aristocrats. Félix Muriel is even permitted to
be much more than a character, becoming at times narrator,
observer, or disappearing completely from the reader's sight.
Narrative and dramatic structure is often loose and open, like that of
life itself. The created work is seen as creating itself, capable of
surprising the characters and even the author.

Behind the varied products of Dieste's pen lies the ontological
concern for the problem of reality and existence which he sees as a
peculiarly Galician vocation, the desire to capture the heart of
reality, not just exterior manifestations. The mystery of self occupies

a central position in all his works, both fiction and nonfiction. He
views man as an unfathomable creature, an unreliable self-witness
in need of additional testimony about his own nature, both
contradictory and complex. Hence the need for human communica-
tions and dialogue, as we see in Anselmo and the hermit Andrés
("The Rock and the Bird"), Don Ramón and Félix Muriel's father
("The Stuffed Parrot"), Don Julián and Félix Muriel ("Pliny's
Garden"), Manuel and David (*Dialogue of Manuel and David*), the
Pilgrim, Don Frontán and the puppeteers (*Journey*), and in
all of these, Rafael Dieste and his reader . . . The
many ways in which we project images of ourselves appear
repeatedly in Dieste's works in the form of masks, mirrors, names,
and words. Sometimes, as in *Perdition of Doña Luparia*, a mirror
serves to reveal unsuspected truths about a person, but most often it
is memory which provides the greatest measure of self-
contemplation because it can illuminate the past with hindsight and
make successive events appear simultaneous. Dieste is always
aware of other views, however, of the antithesis that each thesis
awakens, so that this same memory that liberates (for Félix Muriel)
can also imprison (*Journey, Duel*, "The Stuffed Parrot"). Literary
creation itself is for the author a sort of mirror allowing contemplation of self in others (fellow men) or in alter egos. Even Dieste's
characters frequently choose to observe themselves via plays within
a play (*Journey, Duel*) or by telling stories in which they are
protagonists ("Old Man Moreno," "The Stuffed Parrot").

Opposing the human desire to know oneself is Dieste's realization
that complete knowledge would make us predictable and thus no
longer free, so he celebrates that mystery which surrounds our
being in the world. He tends to view life with a sense of wonder, to
discover anew myths and traditions in "the old skin of the world," to
find marvels in small, familiar things. Manuel's motto "believing is
seeing" shapes the perspective with which Dieste views the
wonders of light, love, nature, and friendship. For that reason,
seemingly unextraordinary situations are capable of yielding profound metaphysical experiences when fired by intuition and
imagination in stories in *From the Goblin's Archives* and *Félix
Muriel* as well as in the author's poetry. As Dieste's studies in
geometry reveal, he is particularly interested in the phenomenon of
movement. This is reflected also in the dynamic quality of his fiction
and poetry, with peripatetic characters who move from place to
place and who also move freely in time by means of memory. His

books on philosophy in dialogue form may be said to have dialectical movement.

Another major concern is the interplay of singularity and universality. Collective, universal history is evoked by mythification and the air of legend and folklore which pervades his fiction, but even in age-old traditions and myths there are new, personalized versions of Pliny, Charlemagne, Celestina, Don Juan, witches and the old man who meets with the devil—all part of the collective heritage. The importance of the collective community is treated in his first play, *The Empty Window*, and appears in his works in the form of Galician people and settings, or more exactly, of communication and harmony between the two. His prose in Spanish bears the lyricism and archaic flavor reminiscent of the Galician vernacular. It frequently waxes baroque with syllogisms and ambiguous turns, but this reflects most adequately the author's attitude toward words as dubious, imperfect, and arbitrary units of expression, though they are the principal means we have by which to recognize ourselves and others.

For this critic Dieste's finest literary achievements to date lie in the plays and in the artistic perfection of his *Félix Muriel*, significantly never revised or changed from the first edition. It seems understandable in view of his circumstances as an emigrant that his interest in writing theater waned, but we would agree with José Marra-López in wishing that Dieste had continued in the narrative vein which produced such fine results in Galician and Spanish.[1] There are writers who are more prolific than Rafael Dieste, but he is self-limiting; he does not publish anything that is not first rate.

The formula for the author's literary magic may be found in a statement regarding the cryptographic aspect of Cubism, but it could be extended to refer also to other expressions of mystery such as symbols, signs, and poetic images. "The cryptographic aspect generally has that power of seduction, not only inquisitive, but also poetic, in that it stimulates the faculty of interpretation and by that route ends up awakening effects of real magical fantasy."[2] Thus the height of artistic attainment would be achieved when the writer or painter's creative faculties are matched by the viewer's intellectual and imaginative responses. It is a philosophy not only for the writer Dieste but also for the reader of his extraordinary literary works.

Notes and References

Chapter One

1. Dieste favors the retention of the Galician spelling which is now widely accepted.
2. Enlarged edition (Buenos Aires, 1940), poem number 30, pp. 62–63.
3. Lecture delivered by Dieste July 17, 1958 in the Cultural Department of *La Razón* (Buenos Aires), reviewed the following day in *La Razón*.

Chapter Two

1. Personal letter from the author.
2. *De Esto y de lo Otro* (La Coruña), 1930.
3. "Respuesta de D. Domingo García Sabell," *A vontade de estilo na fala popular* (La Coruña, 1971), p. 42.
4. *Dos arquivos do trasno*, 3rd ed. (Vigo, 1973). Pages in parentheses are from this edition.
5. Translated from *Les Manifestes du Surréalisme*, Paris, 1946, p. 34.
6. *Phantoms and Fugitives: Journeys to the Improbable* (New York, 1964), p. 130. Translation by Terry Broch Fontseré. The story is from *Todos somos fugitivos*, published in 1961.

Chapter Three

1. The source of this report which appears in the flyleaf of the Buenos Aires edition of 1958 was Ramón Suárez Picallo, eminent lawyer, journalist, and writer, and one of the founders of *Céltiga*, a now defunct Galician journal published in Buenos Aires. Suárez Picallo was a friend of O'Neill's secretary who had been asked by the famous playwright to bring back any especially interesting plays he might hear about while travelling in Spain. One of these works was *The Empty Window*, which he was able to render into English since he knew Galician. This same gentleman communicated to Suárez Picallo the playwright's favorable impression.
2. "Rafael Dieste: En busca de la memoria," *Informaciones* (June 5, 1975), p. 1.
3. *A fiestra valdeira* (Buenos Aires, 1959). Pages in parentheses are from this edition.
4. (Buenos Aires, 1941). Pages in parentheses refer to this edition.

5. *Cuadernos del Laboratorio de Formas de Galicia* (La Coruña, 1975). Pages in parentheses refer to this publication.

6. (Buenos Aires, 1944). The edition, directed by Seoane, was chosen by the American Institute of Graphic Arts and the Pierpont Morgan Library as one of the ten best books in its category published in any country between 1935 and 1945.

Chapter Four

1. "*Viaje, duelo y perdición*, por Rafael Dieste," *Alfar* (Montevideo), 86 (1947).

2. Ibid.

3. *Insula* (Madrid), 211 (June 1964).

4. (Buenos Aires, 1946). Pages in parentheses are from this edition. The titles of the plays are subsequently given in abbreviated form.

5. "A propósito de un libro de Rafael Dieste: *Viaje, duelo y perdición*. Breve exégesis de don Frontán," *Sur* (Buenos Aires), 140 (June 1946).

6. *Así que pasen cinco años, Amor de don Perlimplín con Belisa en su jardín* (Madrid, 1976). Granell convincingly contradicts the traditionally accepted interpretation that Belisa is unfaithful.

7. Juan Gil-Albert, "*Viaje, duelo y perdición*," *Suma Bibliográfica* (Mexico), I, 3 (August 1946).

8. *Alfar*, 86 (1947).

9. Letter dated London, December 21, 1930, published in Eduardo Dieste, *Teseo: Los problemas literarios* (Montevideo, 1938), pp. 197–205 with answer.

10. Information provided by Carmen Muñoz de Dieste in correspondence.

11. Arturo Serrano Plaja, letter to Dieste, Paris, 1946; José Otero Espasandín, *Alfar*, loc. cit.; Juan Gil-Albert, *Suma Bibliográfica*, loc. cit.

12. Ibid.

13. Unsigned article (Buenos Aires, May 12, 1946).

14. *Ramón del Valle Inclán* (New York and London, 1972), p. 45.

Chapter Five

1. *Quebranto de doña Luparia y otras farsas* (Madrid; 1934). Pages are indicated in parentheses.

2. Ibid. Pages are indicated in parentheses.

3. *Hora de España*, XV (March 1938). Pages are indicated in parentheses.

4. Miguel Bilbatúa, editor, *Teatro de agitación política 1933–1939* (Madrid, 1976). Pages in parentheses are from this book. The play was originally published in *Hora de España*, I (January 1937).

The British musicologist and friend of the Dieste's, Albert L. Lloyd, who is widely versed in Spanish letters, translated the play shortly after its publication in *Hora de España*. This translation, entitled "The New Spectacle of Wonders" appeared in *New Writing*, IV (Autumn 1937), 232–44. It is an excellent translation with a decidedly British flavor in the rendering of colloquialisms. We have chosen to translate quotes directly from the Bilbatúa edition because it is more accessible to readers.

5. Eduardo Dieste, *Teseo: Los problemas literarios* (Madrid, 1938), pp. 229–68.

Chapter Six

1. Platea Club, Radio Sténtor. Quoted in flier distributed by Emecé Editores (Buenos Aires), p. 4.

2 *Rojo farol amante* (Buenos Aires, 1940). The numbers in parentheses refer to the numbering of the poems, many of which are untitled in the text.

3. Note provided by the author.

4. "*Viaje, duelo y perdición* por Rafael Dieste," *Suma Bibliográfica*, I, 3 (August 1946).

5. Antonio Machado, "Galerías," LXI. Introducción," *Poesías completas*, 13th ed. (Madrid, 1971), p. 61.

6. "She Walks in Beauty," *Writers of the Western World*, edited by Addison Hibbard and Horst Frenz (Boston, 1954), p. 687.

Chapter Seven

1. Javier Alfaya, "Dieste desperdigado," *Cuadernos para el Diálogo*, No. 129, June 1974.

2. Gimferrer, "Tres escritores solitarios," *Destino* (February 2, 1974); Santos, "Historias e invenciones de Félix Muriel," *Pueblo* (February 27, 1974); Marra-López, *Narradores españoles fuera de España* (Madrid, 1963), p. 485. Among the many critics who reviewed the book in addition to those cited are Manuel Andújar, Enrique Azcoaga, Carlos García Bayón, Esther de Cáceres, Eduardo Dieste, Domingo García-Sabell, Juan Gil-Albert, Miguel González Garcés, Salvador Lorenzana, Joaquín Marco, Ramón Piñeiro, Jorge Rodríguez Padrón, Francisco Umbral, and Lorenzo Varela.

3. (Madrid, 1974). All pages in parentheses are from this edition, which subsequently will be cited as *Félix Muriel*.

4. "*Historias e invenciones de Félix Muriel*," *A. B. C.* (Madrid, March 21, 1974), p. 55.

5. "El rescate de Rafael Dieste," *Triunfo*, 594 (February 16, 1974).

6. Ciudad Trujillo, 1964, and also in *Federica no era tonta y otros cuentos* (Mexico, 1970), pp. 179–84.

7. *"Historias e invenciones de Félix Muriel,"* De Mar a Mar (Buenos Aires), 7 (1943), p. 38.

8. Castroviejo, "Los caminos del recuerdo," *Hoja del Lunes* (Madrid, March 4, 1974) and Suñén, "Historias de Félix Muriel," *Hogar y Pueblo* (Soria, November 4, 1974).

9. *"Historias e invenciones de Félix Muriel,"* Reseña de Literatura, Arte y Espectáculos (Madrid), 74 (April 1974), p. 19.

10. *Triunfo,* loc. cit.

11. Enrique Azcoaga, "Gente de pluma y pincel, *Muriel,"* in author's archives and Luis Suñén, op. cit.

Chapter Eight

1. *Diálogo de Manuel y David y otros ensayos* (Vigo, 1965), p. 11.

2. "La intuición iluminada," prologue to *Testamento geométrico* (La Coruña, 1975), p. 8.

3. "Un libro de Rafael Dieste sobre un problema dos veces milenario," *Galicia Emigrante* (Buenos Aires, June 1957).

4. *Nuevo tratado del paralelismo* (Buenos Aires, 1956), p. 8; subsequent pages are in parentheses.

5. *¿Qué es un axioma?* (Vigo, 1967); pages are in parentheses.

6. *Luchas con el desconfiado* (Buenos Aires, 1948), p. 129. Subsequent references in parentheses.

7. *Historias e invenciones de Félix Muriel,* p. 188.

8. *Diálogo de Manuel y David.* Pages are in parentheses.

9. "*Diálogo de Manuel y David* por Rafael Dieste," *Reseña de Literatura, Arte y Espectáculos,* 11 (February 1966).

10. *La vieja piel del mundo* (Madrid, 1936), p. 36; subsequent pages are in parentheses.

11. Personal letter from author, April 24, 1978.

12. *Pequeña clave ortográfica* (Buenos Aires, 1958), 3rd ed., p. 20.

13. (Buenos Aires, 1941.)

14. *Cuadernos del Laboratorio de Formas de Galicia* (La Coruña, 1975), p. 87; subsequent pages are in parentheses.

Chapter Nine

1. *Narrativa española fuera de España 1939–1961,* p. 486.

2. "La estética pictórica de Carlos Maside," *Cuadernos del Laboratorio de Formas de Galicia* (1975), p. 90.

Selected Bibliography

PRIMARY SOURCES

1. Books

Colmeiro. Breve discurso acerca de pintura con el ejemplo de un pintor.
Buenos Aires: Emecé, 1941.
Diálogo de Manuel y David y otros ensayos. Vigo: Galaxia, Ediciones
Teseo, 1965.
Dos arquivos do trasno. Vigo: El Pueblo Gallego, 1926; revised edition,
Vigo: Galaxia, 1962; definitive edition, Vigo: Galaxia, 1973.
A fiestra valdeira. Santiago, 1927; definitive version, Buenos Aires: Citania,
1959.
Historias e invencións de Félix Muriel. Buenos Aires: Nova, 1943; Madrid:
Alianza Editorial, 1974.
Luchas con el desconfiado. Buenos Aires: Sudamericana, 1948.
Nuevo tratado del paralelismo. Buenos Aires: Atlántida, 1956.
Pequeña clave ortográfica. Buenos Aires: Atlántida, 1956, 1957, 1958,
1963.
¿Qué es un axioma? Vigo: Galaxia, Ediciones Teseo, 1967.
Quebranto de doña Luparia y otras farsas. Madrid: Yague, 1934.
Rojo farol amante. Madrid: Teseo, 1933; enlarged edition, Buenos Aires:
Emede, 1940.
Testamento geométrico. La Coruña: Ediciones del Castro, 1975.
Viaje, duelo y perdición. Tragedia, humorada y comedia. Buenos Aires:
Atlántida, 1945.
Viaje y fin de don Frontán. Santiago: Niké, 1930.
La vieja piel del mundo. Madrid: Signo, 1936.
A vontade de estilo na fala popular. La Coruña: Ediciós do Castro, 1971.

2. Major Writings Included in Other Volumes or Journals
Omitted are articles, essays, and reviews published in *Galicia, El Pueblo
Gallego, Hora de España, Nova Galiza,* and many other periodicals, as
well as lectures, translations, adaptations, and reviews. These items
number in the hundreds and remain to be organized bibliographically.
"Al amanecer," *Hora de España,* XV (March 1938), pp. 99–119.

"La estética pictórica de Carlos Maside, con alusiones a otros pintores coetáneos," *Cuadernos del Laboratorio de Formas de Galicia*, No. 4, La Coruña: Ediciós do Castro, 1975, pp. 81–97, 165–80.

"Nuevo retablo de las maravillas," *Hora de España*, I (January 1937); Miguel Bilbatúa, editor, *Teatro de agitación política*, Madrid: Cuadernos para el Diálogo, 1976, pp. 165–205.

"Pintura ensimismada y fuera de sí." Eduardo Dieste, *Introducción a una lógica del arte*, Madrid: Yagüe, 1934.

"Prólogo." *Homenaje a la Torre de Hércules* (49 drawings by Luis Seoane), Buenos Aires: Nova, 1944.

"Promesa del viejo y de la doncella." Eduardo Dieste, *Teseo: Los problemas literarios*, Montevideo: Reuniones de Estudio, 1938, pp. 229–78 (collaboration with Eduardo Dieste).

"Revelación y rebelión del teatro." *P. A. N.*, No. 1 (1935): Dialogued essay.

"Una semblanza de Buscón poeta." Eduardo Dieste, op. cit., pp. 281–90.

"*Los usurpadores* y *La cabeza del cordero*" *Boletín del Instituto Español* (London), No. 10 (February 1950). On Francisco Ayala.

SECONDARY SOURCES

The following selection represents articles most useful in providing insights into Dieste's writings and person, though most are not analytical studies but rather general surveys and reviews.

1. Articles and Studies of a General Nature

ALFAYA, JAVIER. "Dieste, desperdigado," *Cuadernos para el Diálogo*, No. 129 (June, 1974). Primarily about *Félix Muriel* ("perhaps the best book of stories in the Spanish language in our century"). Treats Dieste's "poetical realism," theater, and stories in Galician briefly.

FABRA BARREIRO, GUSTAVO. "Rafael Dieste: Una recuperación," *Informaciones Literary Supplement*, No. 288 (January 17, 1974), pp. 1, 2. Brief but penetrating survey of Dieste's major works, concentrating on *Félix Muriel* as "novel of voluntary and analytical memory," and suggesting contrasts to Proust.

GARCÍA-SABELL, DOMINGO. "Discurso," in Dieste's *A vontade de estilo na fala popular*, (La Coruña: Ediciós do Castro, 1971), pp. 39–56. The most comprehensive study of Dieste to date, in Galician, touching his major works, emphasizing the poetical rendering of "total reality."

MARRA-LÓPEZ, JOSÉ RAMÓN. "Rafael Dieste," *Narrativa española fuera de España* (1939–1961), Madrid: Guadarrama, 1963, pp. 485–87. Brief presentation of general characteristics with particular praise for *Félix Muriel*. Includes biographical material and bibliography.

NORA, EUGENIO G. DE. *La novela española contemporánea (1927–1939)*, second revised edition, Madrid: Gredos, 1968, pp. 213, 215–16. Observations focus on *Félix Muriel's* atmosphere of mystery and poetry. Comments briefly on subjects, themes, and style.

SEOANE, LUIS. *La Voz de Galicia* (August 30, 1972). Brief but highly revealing personal testimony of Dieste's contributions to Galician culture and influence on notable writers and painters.

2. Published Interviews and Conversations.

FABRA BARREIRO, GUSTAVO. "Rafael Dieste: en busca de la memoria." *Informaciones* (June 5, 1975), pp. 1, 2. Conversations on early years in Galicia, Pedagogical Missions, *Hora de España*, exile, and writing.

MARRA-LÓPEZ, JOSÉ RAMÓN. "Coloquios: Perfil de Rafael Dieste," *Ínsula*, No. 211 (June 1964). Discussions about writing theater and future plans.

PERNAS, MONCHO and ESTÉVEZ, CARLOS. "Rescate de Rafael Dieste," *Triunfo* (June 22, 1974), pp. 50–52. Dieste talks about *Hora de España*, exile, Galician literature, and *Félix Muriel*.

3. Articles and Studies on *Félix Muriel*

ALFARO, JOSÉ MARÍA. "*Historias e invenciones de Félix Muriel*," *A.B.C.*, No. 21 (March 1974), p. 55. Emphasizes its "magic regionalism."

CASTROVIEJO, CONCHA. "Los caminos del recuerdo," *Hoja del Lunes* (March 4, 1974). Excellent treatment of the unifying factor of memory with its power of transformation and discovery.

GIMFERRER, PERE. "Tres escritores solitarios," *Destino* (February 2, 1974). Relates Dieste to the Celtic tradition of the marvelous and calls the volume an "atomized novel."

GÓMEZ MARTÍN, JOSÉ ANTONIO. "Libros: El rescate de Rafael Dieste," *Triunfo*, No. 594 (February 16, 1974). Excellent treatment of "magical realism" and language, "the secret marvel of the book."

MARCO, JOAQUÍN. "Lo maravilloso en la narrativa de Rafael Dieste," *La Vanguardia* (Barcelona, January 31, 1974). Stylistic and aesthetic analysis of Dieste's prose with reference to *Félix Muriel*.

MARTÍN, SALUSTIANO "*Historias e invenciones de Félix Muriel:* Rafael Dieste," *Reseña de Literatura, Arte y Espectáculos*, No. 74 (April 1974). A good article with considerable detail about individual stories, stressing the role of memory and the transition of Félix from narrator to protagonist, attracted by "deep mystery."

RODRÍGUEZ PADRÓN, JORGE. "Encuentro con dos narradores gallegos," *Cuadernos Hispanoamericanos*, No. 300 (June 1975), pp. 674–83. Discusses the stylized utilization of folk material, the handling of time, and the intellectual and symbolical character of the narration. Good insight into the interaction of characters and setting and the search for identity as a major theme.

SERRANO PLAJA, ARTURO. "Libros: *Historias e invenciones de Félix Muriel*, por Rafael Dieste," *De Mar a Mar* (Buenos Aires), No. 7 (1943), pp. 38–40. Good comments on the book's first edition, particularly the discussion of charity as concrete fraternal emotion.

SUÑÉN, LUIS. "Libros: Historias de Félix Muriel," *Hogar y Pueblo* (Soria,

November 20, 1974). A brief but excellent discussion of unifying aspects.

LA VOZ DE GALICIA (February 17, 1974). An issue featuring excellent articles on *Félix Muriel* by Miguel González Garcés, Ramón Piñeiro, Domingo García-Sabell, Marino Dónega, Salvador Lorenzana, and R. Carballo Calero, with several sketches by Luis Seoane from the Argentine edition.

4. Articles and Studies on Other Specific Works

ALTOLAGUIRRE, MANUEL. *"La vieja piel del mundo* por Rafael Dieste," *Hora de España*, No. 1 (January 1937). Brief laudatory review, seeing special relevance in that moment of Civil War and characterizing it as a Nietzschian book of transcendent concerns.

BLANCO TORRES, ROBERTO. "La nueva generación literaria gallega," *De esto y de lo otro*, La Coruña, 1930. Situates Dieste in the panorama of Galician letters as the most outstanding figure of the generation.

GARCÍA-ARMESTO, FERMÍN F. *"¿Qué es un axioma?*, de Rafael Dieste," *La Voz de Galicia* (June 30, 1968). Considers Dieste's mathematical investigations in relation to his more poetical pursuits. With well-chosen quotes, the article provides a clear summary.

GARCÍA-SABELL, DOMINGO. "La intuición iluminada," introductory essay appearing in Dieste's *Testamento geométrico*, pp. 7–13 and in *Insula*, No. 372 (November 1977), p. 11. Clarifies Dieste's attitude toward intuition and reason in pursuing intimate reality.

GIL-ALBERT, JUAN. *"Viaje, duelo y perdición* por Rafael Dieste," *Suma Bibliográfica*, I, No. 3 (August 1946). Briefly contrasts Dieste and Valle-Inclan and compares Don Frontan to heroes like Faust and Don Juan in the grandeur of human destiny.

HOYO, ARTURO DEL. *"La ventana vacía / A fiestra valdeira,"* *Teatro mundial*, Madrid: Aguilar, 1955, p. 285. Presents a summary of the plot with succinct commentary recognizing beauty of language, psychological depth, and a warm sensation of atmosphere.

ITURBURU, CORDOVA. *"Rojo farol amante,"* *La Hora* (Buenos Aires, June 27, 1940). Notes certain affinity with the poetry of Juan Ramón Jiménez but finds atmosphere, symbols, mythology, music, and words quite unique, flowing from interior reflection.

JARNÉS, BENJAMÍN. "Letras españolas," *La Nación* (Buenos Aires, August 16, 1936). Short review of *La vieja piel del mundo* (The Old Skin of the World), pointing out the pursuit of what lies beyond appearances and the projection of man as a historical being in a mythological context.

OTERO-ESPASANDÍN, JOSÉ. "A propósito de un libro de Rafael Dieste: *Viaje, duelo y perdición:* Breve exégesis de Don Frontán," *Sur*, No. 140 (June 1946). Presents a very subjective and lyrical view of the play, suggesting mythical flavor and eternal roots. The critic perceives a profound Galician spirit in the work.

_____. "*Viaje, duelo y perdición* por Rafael Dieste," *Alfar* (Montevideo), No. 86 (1947). Discusses the revision of earlier versions. The critic finds no equal to Dieste's theater since Golden Age Spain and contrasts his work to the overly-sweet "lyrical theater" current at the time.

SOBEJANO, GONZALO. *Nietzsche en España*, Madrid: Editorial Gredos, 1967, pp. 649–50. Brief comments on *The Old Skin of the World* providing a clear summary with well-chosen, quotes. Considers the "style of intellectual play tending toward fictions and allegories" as prewar.

TORRES QUEIRUGA, ANDRÉS. "*Diálogo de Manuel y David* por Rafael Dieste," *Reseña de Literatura, Arte y Espectáculos*, No. 11 (February 1966) Good schematic review of Dieste's varied production, finding a common denominator of fine aesthetic sensitivity revealed in symbols and poetic play. Traces in broad terms the themes of the essay and Dieste's respect for that which cannot be known.

ZAID, GABRIEL. "Un libro de Rafael Dieste sobre un problema dos veces milenario," *Galicia Emigrante* (Buenos Aires, June 1957). The critic, a writer and engineer, is particularly qualified to discuss the contribution of *New Treatise on Parallelism* in opening new horizons for the conception of space and for methods of investigation. Also observes the essential unity of all Dieste's writings.

Index

(The works of Dieste are listed under his name)